# Literacy as Snake Oil

new
literacies
¶

AND DIGITAL EPISTEMOLOGIES

Colin Lankshear, Michele Knobel,
Chris Bigum, and Michael Peters
*General Editors*

Vol. 1

PETER LANG
New York • Washington, D.C./Baltimore • Bern
Frankfurt am Main • Berlin • Brussels • Vienna • Oxford

# Literacy as Snake Oil

## Beyond the Quick Fix

*dxxt*

EDITED BY
## Joanne Larson

PETER LANG
New York • Washington, D.C./Baltimore • Bern
Frankfurt am Main • Berlin • Brussels • Vienna • Oxford

**Library of Congress Cataloging-in-Publication Data**

Literacy as snake oil: beyond the quick fix / edited by Joanne Larson.
p. cm. — (New literacies and digital epistemologies; vol. 1)
Includes bibliographical references and index.
1. Literacy programs—United States. I. Larson, Joanne. II. Series.
LC151 .L4815  372.6'0973—dc21  00-067151
ISBN 0-8204-5021-9
ISSN 1523-9543


**Die Deutsche Bibliothek-CIP-Einheitsaufnahme**

Literacy as snake oil: beyond the quick fix / ed. by: Joanne Larson.
–New York; Washington, D.C./Baltimore; Bern;
Frankfurt am Main; Berlin; Brussels; Vienna; Oxford: Lang.
(New literacies and digital epistemologies; Vol. 1)
ISBN 0-8204-5021-9

Cover art courtesy of Strong Museum, Rochester, New York © 2001.
Cover design by Lisa Dillon


The paper in this book meets the guidelines for permanence and durability
of the Committee on Production Guidelines for Book Longevity
of the Council of Library Resources.

**Table of Contents**

# Series Foreword

Colin Lankshear, Michele Knobel, Michael Peters

Educators around the world are struggling to understand and develop effective and principled responses to deep and far-reaching social, economic, cultural, political, and technological changes that have been developing since the 1950s. This series hopes to contribute to this struggle by addressing two manifestations of these changes that go to the very heart of educational work.

The first is the emergence of diverse new literacies embedded in evolving and emerging social practices associated with contemporary change. Many, but by no means *all* of these new literacies, are mediated by new electronic information and communications technologies. Others—such as those addressed in the present volume—are responses to pubic perceptions that schools are finding it increasingly difficult to ensure literacy for all at the precise historical moment when the information revolution, a diminished welfare state, and an emerging knowledge economy are upping the ante for literacy. Within this context a wealth of commodified packaged literacies have appeared on the educational quick-fix market.

The second focus of the series is on digital epistemologies. This idea that contemporary changes are generating new kinds of phenomena to be known and understood, and are calling for new conceptions of knowledge, new approaches to knowing, and a new balance between different kinds of knowledge. In particular, the conventional epistemology of "justified true belief" that has dominated Western thought since the time of Plato and underpinned the subject discipline-based curriculum of school education since its inception, is profoundly undermined by changes associated with the explosion of new information and communications technologies.

Much of what passes for knowledge in cyberspace as well as in what Lyotard calls the postmodern condition does not have to be true. It may not even be important that a body of knowledge be believed by those who use it. It is most likely that the emphasis on prepositional knowledge inherent in the underlying epistemology of school education will increasingly be displaced by a "performance epistemology" attuned to originality and innovation. Furthermore, in the context of proliferating distributed and networked communities of knowledge practice, and escalating use of diverse kinds of information services, "bots", and other "intelligent agents" in knowledge work, the Cartesian image of the individual cognizing and knowing subject presumed by school education has been displaced.

The series aims to promote awareness of such issues associated with contemporary change within mainstream educational thinking and to help encourage appropriate and principled responses in educational theory and practice. The series will challenge familiar ways of thinking and acting in education, and provide a forum for exploring innovative, unusual, and risky ideas and perspectives in the areas of new literacies and digital epistemologies.

*Literacy as Snake Oil* explores the current fetish for packaged literacy materials as a strategy for pursuing acceptable levels of learning outcomes in a milieu of standards-based accountability. The book assembles a truly impressive team of literacy scholars ideally placed to develop an active, critical stance in exposing the consequences of commodified literacy on educational practice. An important strength of the book is that it moves beyond critique as merely a form of oppositional practice to intensified commodification of literacy. In addition, it advances a wide range of constructive and useful ideas and experiences that will be of much interest to teacher educators' concerns with teaching 'what we know about literacy (as socio cultural practice) in the context of standardization and accountability' (p. 1).

# Acknowledgments

This book would not have been possible without the help of several dedicated people. I am indebted to Colin Lankshear and Michele Knobel for entrusting me with this project. I want to thank the distinguished scholars who contributed their insights to this volume. Their research and experience in literacy teaching and learning are invaluable to gaining a deeper understanding of the critical issues in literacy education. The Warner School's faculty secretary, Shirley Graham, worked tirelessly on preparing the manuscript for publication and I am grateful for her time and effort. My graduate research assistant, Gloria Jacobs, provided careful readings of the final draft. Finally, I want to thank my husband, Morris Smith, for his enduring love and support and my three children, Anna, Eric, and Marcus, for always reminding me why this work is important.

## Chapter One

# In Sheep's Clothing: Literacy for Sale

*Joanne Larson*

The purpose of this book is to critically examine the recent trend toward quick-fix literacy programs in which commodified literacy is peddled by entrepreneurs seeking to solve what they are calling the current reading crisis. Literacy scholars who are researching and writing about these issues come together in this volume to offer in-depth analyses of the problem of commodified literacies. The book is intended for teacher educators who themselves are struggling with how to teach what we know about literacy learning in the context of standardization and accountability. This introductory chapter will provide a brief overview of current issues in literacy education, focusing specifically on the larger context within which packaged literacy programs have emerged. In addition, this chapter will briefly describe the contents of the book.

The reality of current accountability and standardization movements both locally and nationally that feeds the market for packaged literacies makes this an important and timely book. Furthermore, recent questions about why researchers of literacy as a social practice and critical literacy are not included in public policy conversations about curriculum, pedagogy, and assessment makes understanding the emergence and consequences of the commodification of literacy crucial to shifting from a defensive position to one that is proactive. In the United States, in particular, the conservative right has successfully fueled fears about the declining skills of American students in the global marketplace. Scholars using this argument cite "scientific evidence" as the basis for their argument in favor of a skills-only approach (Coles, 2000). Furthermore, research on basic skills instruction, which has been shown to be based in controversial assumptions about ability and intelligence, has resulted in the banning of contextualized literacy instruction in favor of phonics-only instructional packages (Coles, 2000; Taylor, 1998).

Educational researchers, policymakers, administrators, and teachers struggling to deal with recent standardization and accountability pressures focus primarily on improving achievement rather than critically examining the larger context that is motivating the drive for standardization. In literacy education, the obsession with the so-called great debate has polarized public discourse into antagonistic arguments over which method works best. Recent calls for moving beyond the debate issue challenge us to construct more critical understandings of what must be done to ensure that all children learn literacy.

The so-called reading crisis is currently instantiated as the reading wars (Goodman, 1998), the never-ending debate between meaning-based philosophy and basic skills instruction. In its current instantiation, the argument goes back and forth between contextualized, whole text instruction and systematic, explicit phonics instruction. As literacy educators, we have seen this kind of scholarly debate between whole text and the alphabetic principle for over one hundred years (Langer & Allington, 1992). In spite of calls to end this constant one upmanship, the argument continues (c.f. *Educational Researcher*, August/September 2000).

Gerald Coles (1998) has argued that the "Great Debate is the wrong debate" and adds that most of the debate about literacy fails to take into account the many influences outside the classroom which affect literacy teaching and learning. While instruction is important, he argues, narrow questions about methods "do nothing to address the deeper causes of literacy problems...in all their political, empirical, professional and instructional permutations" (1998, p. 21). Allan Luke (1998) called for a reframing of the debate over methods, pointing out that the social practice of literacy is always affected by the larger political and economic conditions. The current political context of standardization and accountability puts teacher educators, teachers, and administrators in the difficult position of trying to make sense of these issues. Profit-oriented publishing houses have responded by producing "scientifically proven" techniques that they promise will fix the reading crisis.

Teachers tend to fall back on their existing beliefs and practices, citing the oft heard "pendulum swing" excuse as their reason for ignoring district mandates or simply following the directions in new packaged literacy materials. It is hard to blame them given the pressure to hold them accountable for student achievement. Their jobs are at stake. They are bombarded by their district administrators and by advertising in professional literature with commercially produced materials that promise new and improved literacy outcomes. By relying on commercially produced materials, teachers and administrators can shift responsibility to the materials and the reason for continued underachievement to students.

The survival of teaching as a profession requires us to get beyond quick-fix solutions. To assume a quick fix is possible is to assume that teaching itself is simply a matter of technique. The nearer teaching gets to machine-like behavior the more readily it can be displaced; the more deskilled it becomes, the less bargaining power teachers have as a profession (Lankshear, personal communication). This book does not argue for new and improved methods, or quick fixes, but presents carefully reasoned discussions that will help teacher educators, classroom teachers, and school administrators understand the consequences of commercially produced literacy packages, or commodified literacy, on literacy learning.

## Overview of the Book

In chapter two, James Paul Gee analyzes the 1998 National Research Council report called *Preventing Reading Difficulties in Young Children*. The report is part of a much larger academic and public debate in the 1980s and 1990s over reading and reading instruction in the schools. This report, like many others, was quite well received by professional organizations, the media, and the public. In fact, it sought in part to end debates around reading by stating what it claimed was an emerging consensus in the field of reading. Though there have been other such reports and more will follow, the National Research Council's report is, in many ways, the best of its kind. It fairly summarizes the research on reading and is less "dogmatic" than other recent reading policy documents. Given that the report was, indeed, well received—not least by much of the reading profession—Gee will not so much interrogate its claims directly, but its silences and paradoxes, silences and paradoxes which, nonetheless, call into question a number of the report's direct claims. Gee believes the silences and paradoxes of the report represent the silences and paradoxes inside a good many of the recent and current discussions of reading. Gee interrogates these silences and paradoxes to suggest what reports like this one might have been like had they been dedicated not to "reading" as a field in its own right, but to a broader notion of multiple literacies and social practices in schools and society, especially schools and societies facing the "new times" of our emerging high-tech global economy (Gee, Hull, & Lankshear, 1996).

Gee begins by first pointing to salient silences and paradoxes in the report involving such issues as how to define the "reading problem" in the U.S., the relationship between poverty and reading, the role of phonological awareness in preventing reading difficulties, the nature of language as a functional system as against a biologically specified design, and arguments for direct instruction in reading. Then he will briefly discuss how a broader notion of reading—really a notion of literacy as multiple, situated, social, and cultural—would have better spoken to these silences and helped to resolve some of these paradoxes. In the end, he raises the possibility that the National Research Council's report, like others of its kind, seeks to assert simplistic "quick fixes" to a "reading problem" as a way of avoiding naming much deeper problems and discussing much deeper economic, social, institutional, and cultural issues occurring across the world and in the U.S. as part and parcel of the new global capitalism and the current hegemony of neoliberalism.

Building on his discussion of the National Reading Council's report in *Misreading Reading: The Bad Science That Hurts Children* (2000), Gerald Coles examines the constitution of the reading panel as a biased entity whose conclusions were in line with the National Institute of Child Health and Human Development's predisposition toward direct, explicit, systematic instruction of skills. The chapter continues with a critique of the meta-analytic approach taken by the panel and a close analysis of five of the studies described in the report. He concludes with a call for teachers to undertake a countering of what he calls "pseudoscience," which has been undermining the valuable role science might play in advancing literacy teaching and learning.

In chapter four, Patricia Irvine and Joanne Larson explore how elementary teachers in an urban district serving predominantly low-income African-American and Latino students incorporate commodified literacy materials in their instructional practices. Defining commodified literacy materials as those materials purchased by schools from profit-oriented publishing corporations, Irvine and Larson describe how teachers used the materials selectively, choosing activities that reflected deficit ideologies about students' language and abilities. They describe a study of a basal reading series pilot and present data to show that the "autonomous" definition of literacy (Street, 1995) that underlies the materials, in combination with a deficit model of students' abilities, resulted in pedagogical practices that academically disadvantaged students.

Chapter five describes what fourth grade teacher Lynn Astarita Gatto struggles with while trying to construct meaningful pedagogy in her urban classroom. Gatto is a teacher in the same district described by Irvine and Larson and is bombarded with commercially produced materials mandated by the central office administration. This chapter outlines what she does and how she avoids using these materials.

In chapter six, Patrick Shannon examines the commodification of both virtue and literacy embedded in the efforts of William Bennett's attempts to civilize Americans. Since 1994, Bennett has written, edited, or collaborated on four books, five anthologies for adults and children, six collections for children, a PBS cartoon series, and a popular Internet Website in order "to overcome the consequences of the 1960s." Shannon not only addresses Bennett's intentions for Americans and the contents of his wares, he examines how Bennett has used philanthropic, corporate, and government funding to ensure that his message dominates the public struggle over virtue in the U.S. Shannon's hope with these efforts is to suggest that commodification is a historical consequence of capitalism, which is running its natural course in the 1990s without effective opposition from other historic groups which are disadvantaged under this social system. He will end with some thoughts on where that opposition might start and how it might happen.

In chapter seven, Kris D. Gutierrez examines how anti-immigrant and educational reform policies in California have come together to influence the teaching and learning of literacy for urban elementary school children. Drawing on studies of effective practice and, more recently, the effects of Proposition 227, the English-only policy, Gutierrez documents the ways language ideology is instantiated in school policies and classroom practices. In particular, she tells the stories of several classrooms where children's primary literacy experiences and practices could no longer serve as resources for learning.

In the final chapter, Brian Brent argues that those who make school policy (politicians, bureaucrats, and administrators) do so in an effort to increase educational productivity. Many literacy programs, for example, promise to reduce costs and increase student learning; a desirable result for any school official who has been called on to increase student learning despite declining budgets. Brent discusses the processes and dynamics of how school officials and others develop policies that promote the purchase of packaged literacy programs. In addition, he critiques administrators' reliance on these programs by questioning assumptions they make about the relationship between purchased programs and educational productivity. Specifically, Brent demonstrates that the mistake is not one of applying economic concepts to education but of applying them badly. Second, and more importantly, Brent presents a framework that administrators and teachers can use to determine whether a given literacy program is likely to succeed or fail, before it is implemented. Such a framework can be used to escape a siren's call to adopt a quick-fix literacy program.

# References

Coles, G. (1998). *Reading Lessons: The Debate Over Literacy.* New York: Hill and Wang.

Coles, G. (2000). *Misreading Reading: The Bad Science That Hurts Children.* Portsmouth, NH: Heinemann.

Gee, J.P., Hull, G., & Lankshear, C. (1996). *The New Work Order: Behind The Language Of The New Capitalism.* Sydney: Allen & Unwin.

Goodman, K. (1998). *In Defense Of Good Teaching.* York, ME: Stenhouse.

Langer, J., & Allington, R. (1992). "Curriculum Research In Writing And Reading." In P. Jackson (Ed.), *Handbook Of Research On Curriculum.* New York: Macmillan. (pp. 687–725).

Luke, A. (1998). "Getting Over Method: Literacy Teaching As Work In "New Times," *Language Arts, 75*(4), (pp. 305–313).

Street, B. (1995). *Social Literacies: Critical Approaches to Literacy in Development, Ethnography and Education.* London: Longman.

Taylor, D. (1998). *Beginning To Read And The Spin Doctors Of Science: The Political Campaign To Change America's Mind About How Children Learn To Read.* Urbana, IL: National Council of Teachers of English.

# Chapter Two

## Reading, Language Abilities, and Semiotic Resources: Beyond Limited Perspectives on Reading

*James Paul Gee*

### Introduction

Gerald Coles, in his book *Misreading Reading: The Bad Science That Hurts Children* (2000), and Denny Taylor, in her book *Beginning to Read and the Spin Doctors of Science* (1998), do about as good a job as can be imagined debunking the so-called "scientific research" that has fueled calls—in the media, public policy documents, and state legislation (especially in Texas and California)—for scripted direct instruction in phonics and related areas of literacy. There is no point in rehashing their critique here. Rather, I want to argue that the current debates over reading are misplaced—that is, that they systematically evade more important and central issues to focus on an overly narrow perspective on reading and early instruction. In turn, I argue that this narrow perspective fits with the current neoliberal political agenda in the United States (and most of the developed world) and reinforces the growing disparities in wealth, access, and equity in our "new capitalist," neoliberal, global world.

In developing my discussion I will use the relatively recent report on reading from the National Research Council, an arm of the National Academy of Sciences, as a "thinking tool." This report—*Preventing Reading Difficulties in Young Children* (Snow, Burns, & Griffin, 1998)—appeared amidst much applause and approval from the public, politicians, and educational organizations like American Educational Research Association, International Reading Association, and National Council of Teachers of English, organizations which, by and large, with some dissenting voices, celebrated the report in newsletters and sessions. The report is, in some respects, typical of recent public policy documents in early reading, though it is, in fact, better than most in being a bit broader and a bit more evenhanded in its summary of research. Indeed, it is this very (relative) evenhandedness that leads to difficulties (in my view) in the report, since, at various points, the report's comments on relevant research come close to contradicting some of its descriptive claims and policy proposals (Gee, 1999a).

After discussing the National Academy's report, as a way to point out the narrow perspective taken on reading in recent public discussion and the evasions that such a narrow perspective enacts, I will turn to a broader view of reading. I will then close this chapter on a discussion of early "literacies"—literacies that go far beyond learning to decode—that, I believe, underlie school success, especially for upper-middle-class children. The overall point I want to make in this chapter is that from early on in school our focus ought to be not on reading, and especially not on reading as a decontextualized act, but on learning that will translate to success from kindergarten through college and life (Bransford & Schwartz, 1999). I believe that only this sort of focus can really address issues of access, equity, and equality. In the context of our current high-tech, global "new capitalism," a focus on early learning that translates to later learning is more crucial than it has ever been before.

## The National Academy of Sciences' Report

While the National Academy's report discusses a wide range of issues relevant to reading and classroom instruction, it devotes the lion's share of its focus to the importance of early phonemic awareness and sustained overt instruction on "phonics" for learning what the report calls "real reading." In a quick survey of the report's index, categories concerned with sound, decoding, and word recognition take up nearly as many headings and subheadings as all categories concerned with society, culture, families, poverty, race, comprehension, reading stories, narrative, language, learning, development, and related terms, combined (by my count, 3 of 244 headings and subheadings for the former and 275 for the latter).

The report defines "real reading" (as opposed, for instance, to emergent literacy) as decoding, word recognition, and comprehension of literal meaning of text, with a focus on phonemic awareness and the phonological-graphemic code. Thus, for this report, a child who is using multiple cues for word recognition (e.g., decoding, meaning, syntax, and pictures), rather than using just decoding for recognition, relegating other cues to checking words that have been initially recognized by decoding, is not "really reading," but, presumably, still engaged in some form of emergent literacy.

As I have indicated above, the National Academy's report is but one of a number of public policy documents that have dealt with early reading with a significant (though not necessarily exclusive) focus on early phonemic awareness and direct instruction on phonics. What renders the report odd and paradoxical, as well as a good many other such documents, is, I believe, this: "reading" in the sense in which the report discusses the term does not "really" exist. To develop this idea, I will first offer a critique of the Academy's report. I will then return to why I believe reading in the sense the report discusses it, does not exist and what does exist in its stead.

## What's the Crisis?

The Academy's report is part of a long line of reports written in the now familiar "we have a crisis in our schools" genre. Unfortunately, the report has a hard time naming the crisis to which it is directed. Its authors are well aware there is, in fact, no "reading crisis" in the United States:

> ...average reading achievement has not changed markedly over the last 20 years (NAEP, 1997). And following a gain by black children from 1970 to 1980, the white-black gap has remained roughly constant for the last 16 years.
> ...Americans do very well in international comparisons of reading—much better, comparatively speaking, than they do on math or science. In a 1992 study comparing reading skill levels among 9 year-olds in 18 Western nations, U.S. students scored among the highest levels and were second only to students in Finland ... (Elley, 1992, pp.97–98).

There is here, of course, the hint of paradox. The report does not take note of how odd it is (or what implications it might have for reading) that a country could do very well in reading, but poorly in content areas like math and science. For the writers of the report, it is as if content (things like math and science) has nothing to do with reading and *vice versa*.

However, this paradox is endemic to the report as a whole. Note the report's remarks on the much discussed issue of the "fourth-grade drop off."

> The "fourth-grade slump" is a term used to describe a widely encountered disappointment when examining scores of fourth graders in comparison to younger children (Chall et al., 1990). ... It is not clear what the explanation is or even that there is a unitary explanation (p. 78).

The fourth-grade drop-off problem is precisely the problem that lots of children learn to read in the early grades, but then cannot read to learn anything with content in the later grades. The fourth-grade drop-off problem would, on the face of it, lead one to worry about what we mean by "learning to read" in the early grades and how and why this idea can become so detached from "reading to learn." No such worries plague the Academy's report. It assumes though that if children learn to engage in what the report calls "real reading" they will thereafter be able to learn and succeed in school. But the fourth-grade drop-off problem amply demonstrates that this assumption is false.

The report's somewhat cavalier attitude toward the content of reading (that is toward reading as reading *something*, rather than as reading generically to develop "reading skills") can be seen, as well, in the following remark that the report makes about comprehension:

> Tracing the development of reading comprehension to show the necessary and sufficient conditions to prevent reading difficulty is not as well researched as other aspects of reading growth. In fact, as Cain (1996) notes, "because early reading instruction emphasizes word recognition rather than comprehension, the less skilled comprehenders' difficulties generally go unnoticed by their classroom teachers" (p. 77).

Note the paradox here: The report acknowledges Cain's claim that we know too little about comprehension difficulties because research has concentrated on word recognition, but then the report goes on blithely to concentrate on decoding and word recognition, as if we can safely ignore our ignorance about difficulties in comprehension and make recommendations about reading instruction in the absence of such knowledge. Of course, the report does call for teaching comprehension skills, but the teaching it calls for is all generic (things like summarizing or asking oneself questions while reading). It is not rooted in any details about learning specific genres and practices and certainly not about learning different sorts of content (e.g., science, literature, or math).

Yet reading (and, for that matter, speaking) always and only occurs within specific practices and within specific genres in the service of specific purposes or content. And, indeed, it is precisely children's difficulties with using language and literacy within specific practices and genres that fuels the fourth-grade drop off. The worldwide genre movements, which have stressed this fact about literacy and its myriad implications for pedagogy, go virtually unreferenced in the Academy's report (Berkenkotter & Huckin, 1994; Christie, 1990; Cope & Kalantzis, 1993; Freedman & Medway, 1994; Martin, 1998).

## Reading, Racism, and Poverty

The Academy's report is well aware that, in the United States, poor readers are concentrated "in certain ethnic groups and in poor, urban neighborhoods and rural towns" (p. 98). In fact, this is the true "crisis" in reading in the United States, though one the report never focuses on. Here, too, we are faced with paradoxes. Let us return to the quote from the report with which we started:

> ...average reading achievement has not changed markedly over the last 20 years (NAEP, 1997). And following a gain by black children from 1970 to 1980, the white-black gap has remained roughly constant for the last 16 years.
> ...Americans do very well in international comparisons of reading—much better, comparatively speaking, than they do on math or science. In a 1992 study comparing reading skill levels among 9 year-olds in 18 Western nations, U.S. students scored among the highest levels and were second only to students in Finland ... (Elley, 1992, pp. 97–98).

Here the report mentions the now well-known and much studied issue that from the late 1960s to the early 1980s, the Black-White gap in IQ test scores and other sorts of test scores, including reading tests, was fast closing (Neisser, 1998; Jencks & Phillips, 1998). This heartening progress, especially in regard to achievement tests, ceased in the 1980s. One certainly would have thought that a reading report would care deeply about the factors that had been closing the Black-White gap in reading scores. Clearly, these factors were, whatever else they were, powerful "reading interventions," since they significantly increased the reading scores of "at risk" children. But the report shows no such interest, presumably because these factors were social and cultural and factors only narrowly germane to classroom instructional methods.

Though the matter is controversial (Neisser, 1998; Jencks & Phillips, 1998), these factors were, in all likelihood, closely connected to the sorts of social programs (stemming originally from Johnson's "War on Poverty") that were dismantled in the 1980s and 1990s (Grissmer, Flanagan, & Williamson, 1998, pp. 221–223). An approach like the Academy's that sees the key issue as "real reading" is not liable to see such social programs as central to a report on reading. Ironically though, the progress made on reading tests during the time the Black-White gap was closing was far greater, in quantitative terms (Hedges & Nowell, 1998), than the report discusses and advocates.

The following remarks from the report are typical of the sense of paradox bordering on outright contradiction that pervades the report on the issue of poor and minority children:

> ...for students in schools in which more than 75 percent of all students received free or reduced-price lunches (measure of high poverty), the mean score for students in the fall semester of first grade was at approximately the

44th percentile. By the spring of third grade, this difference had expanded
significantly. Children living in high poverty areas tend to fall further behind,
regardless of their initial reading skill level (p. 98).

If these children fall further and further behind "regardless of their
initial reading skill level," how, then, can we help them by increasing
their initial skill level at "real reading" through things like early
phonemic awareness and overt instruction on decoding, as the report
recommends?

Finally, we reach the issues of racism and power. It is widely
believed that such issues are "merely political," not directly relevant to
reading and reading research. The Academy's report is certainly written
in such a spirit. But the fact of the matter is that racism and power are
just as much cognitive issues as they are political ones. Children will not
identify with—they will even misidentify with—teachers and schools
that they perceive as hostile, alien, or oppressive to their home-based
identities (Holland & Quinn, 1987; Holland, Lachicotte, Skinner, &
Cain, 1998).

Claude Steele's (Steele, 1992; Steele and Aronson, 1995, 1998)
groundbreaking work clearly demonstrates that in assessment contexts
where issues of race, racism, and stereotypes are triggered, the
performance of even quite adept learners seriously deteriorates (see
Ferguson, 1998, for an important extension of Steele's work). Steele
shows clearly that how people *read* when they are taking tests changes as
their fear of falling victim to cultural stereotypes increases. To ignore
these wider issues, while stressing such things as phonemic awareness on
controlled texts, is to ignore, not merely "politics," but what we know
about learning and literacy, as well.

In fact, one can go further. Given Steele's work, it is simply wrong
to discuss reading assessment, intervention, and instruction, as the
Academy's report does, without discussing the pervasive *culture of
inequality* that deskills poor and minority children and its implications
for different types of assessments, interventions, and instruction. This is
an empirical point, not (only) a political one.

The Academy's report does not define the "reading crisis" as a crisis
of inequality, though it might well have done so. Rather aware, as it is,
that reading scores are not declining among the vast majority of the
student population, the report takes the now fashionable tack that the
"reading crisis" is really due to the increased demands for higher-level
literacy in our technologically driven society:

> Of course, most children learn to read fairly well. In this report, we are
> most concerned with the large numbers of children in America whose
> educational careers are imperiled because they do not read well enough to

ensure understanding and to meet the demands of an increasingly competitive economy. Current difficulties in reading largely originate from rising demands for literacy, not from declining absolute levels of literacy. In a technological society, the demands for higher literacy are ever increasing, more grievous consequences for those who fall short (p. 1).

While this is a common argument today, it ignores the fact that modern science and technology, in fact, create many jobs in which literacy demands go down, not up, thanks to human skills being replaced by computers and other sorts of technological devices (Aronowitz & DiFazio, 1994; Carnoy, Castells, Cohen, & Cardoso, 1993; Mishel & Teixeira, 1991). This is true not just for service sector jobs, but also for many higher status jobs in areas like engineering and bioscience. Indeed, there is much controversy today as to which category is larger: jobs where science and technology have increased literacy demands or those where they have decreased them.

This remark, like the report as a whole, also ignores the fact that in our technologically driven society, literacy is changing dramatically. What appears to be crucial for success now are abilities to deal with multimodal texts (texts that mix words and images), nonverbal symbols, and with technical systems within specific, and now usually highly collaborative, institutional practices. The Academy's report doggedly focuses on reading at the "Dick and Jane" level (albeit with, perhaps, more interesting texts), while calling for students who are prepared to work in the twenty-first century. In the coming world, we are going to face not just a fourth-grade drop-off problem, but a "life drop off problem," as people at every age fail to be able to keep up with fast-paced change requiring multiple new literacies. The Academy's report pales to near insignificance in this context—ironically the only context in which the report acknowledges that we have a "reading crisis." My discussion of language abilities in the next section is relevant as well to this matter.

## Language Abilities

It is a deep irony that a report that spends most of its time recommending early phonemic awareness and early sustained and overt instruction on phonics is replete with comments that appear to undermine its recommendations. For example, consider the following remarks from the report:

...studies indicate that training in phonological awareness, particularly in association with instruction in letters and letter-sound relationships, make a contribution to assisting at risk children in learning to read. The effects of training, although quite consistent, are only moderate in strength, and have so far not been shown to extend to comprehension. Typically a majority of the trained children narrow the gap between themselves and initially more advanced students in phonological awareness and word reading skills, but few are brought completely up to speed through training, and a few fail to show any gains at all (p. 251).

When classificatory analyses are conducted, phonological awareness in kindergarten appears to have the tendency to be a more successful predictor of future superior reading than of future reading problems (Wagner, 1997; Scarborough, 1998). That is, among children who have recently begun or will soon begin kindergarten, few of those with strong phonological awareness skills will stumble in learning to read, but many of those with weak phonological sensitivity will go on to become adequate readers.

In sum, despite the theoretical importance of phonological awareness for learning to read, its predictive power is somewhat muted, because, at about the time of the onset of schooling, so many children who will go on to become normally achieving readers have not yet attained much, if any, appreciation of the phonological structure of oral language, making them nearly indistinguishable in this regard from children who will indeed encounter reading difficulties down the road (p. 112).

There would seem to be an important theme here, one to which the Academy's panel might have paid a bit more heed. Tests of early phonological awareness (or lack thereof ) do not fruitfully select those students who will later have problems in learning to read. Furthermore, while a stress on phonological awareness and overt phonics instruction does initially help "at risk" students, it does not bring them up to par with more advantaged students, and they tend to eventually fall back, fueling a fourth-grade or later "slump" (this fact is amply documented in the report, see pp. 216, 228, 232, 248–249, 251, 257).

From remarks like those above, it would certainly seem that the problems children (particularly poor and minority children) have with reading must lay, for the most part, someplace else than on a lack of early phonemic awareness. The fourth-grade drop off tells us this much, as well. Though much of the Academy's report is driven by the correlation between early phonological awareness and later success in learning to read, the report does readily acknowledge that such a correlation does not prove that phonological awareness causes success in reading. And, indeed, remarks from the report like those cited above, and the fourth-grade drop-off problem itself, would seem to indicate that something else causes *both* reading success (or failure) and early phonemic awareness (or lack of it).

The report is, ironically, aware of what this something else might be. It readily acknowledges, but ignores the fact, that another correlation is just as significant (if not more so) as that between early phonological awareness and learning to read. This is the correlation between *early language abilities* and later success in reading. And, as one might suspect, early language abilities and early phonological awareness are themselves correlated:

> Chaney (1992) also observed that performance on phonological awareness tasks by preschoolers was highly correlated with general language ability. Moreover it was measures of semantic and syntactic skills, rather than speech discrimination and articulation, that predicted phonological awareness differences (p. 53).

> What is most striking about the results of the preceding studies is the power of early preschool language to predict reading three to five years later (pp. 107–108). On average, phonological awareness (r. = .46) has been about as strong a predictor of future reading as memory for sentences and stories, confrontation naming, and general language measures (p. 112).

It is something of a mystery—at least to me—why the Academy's report stresses throughout the correlation between early phonemic awareness and learning to read, while giving such short shrift to early language abilities, a factor that seems to have so much more relevance to both becoming literate and being able to use literacy to learn. One can only suspect that it was the urge to make the Academy's report a "report on reading," and to speak within the frame of current public debates about reading, that led the Academy's panel in the direction it took toward early phonological awareness and phonics and away from early language abilities.

So what are these early language abilities that seem so important for later success in school? According to the report, they are things like vocabulary—receptive vocabulary, but more especially expressive vocabulary (p. 107)—the ability to recall and comprehend sentences and stories, and the ability to engage in verbal interactions. Furthermore, I think that research has made it fairly clear what causes such verbal ability. What appears to cause enhanced verbal abilities are family, community, and school language environments in which children interact intensively with adults and more advanced peers and experience cognitively challenging talk and texts on sustained topics and in different genres of oral and written language (see pp. 106–108).

However, the correlation between language abilities and success in learning to read (and in school generally) hides an important reality.

Almost all children—including poor children—have impressive language abilities. The vast majority of children enter school with large vocabularies, complex grammar, and deep understandings of experiences and stories. It has been decades since anyone believed that poor and minority children entered school with "no language" (Labov, 1972; Gee, 1996).

The verbal activities that children who fail in school fail to have are not just some general set of such abilities, but rather specific verbal abilities tied to specific school-based practices and school-based genres of oral and written language. So, we are back, once again, to where we started: reading something, that is, reading a specific genre for specific purposes within a specific activity, and not reading generically. The children whose vocabularies are larger in ways that enhance their early school success, for instance, are children who know, and especially can use, more words tied to the specific forms of language that school-based practices use. A stress on language abilities would have required an emphasis on learning, content, and the relationships between home-based cultures and school-based practices (i.e., social, cultural, and, yes, "political" issues).


## Reading Versus Reading Something

I said at the outset that what I believed made the Academy's report paradoxical is that "reading" in the sense in which the report discusses the term doesn't really exist. That itself sounds paradoxical, so let me explicate what I mean.

There is no such thing as "reading" *simpliciter*. When we read—child or adult—we always read *something*. This something is always a text of *a certain type* (in a certain genre) and is read (interpreted) *in a certain way*. What makes a text a certain type of text (e.g., a piece of literature, a reading test passage, an "educational" book, a piece of language play, and so on and so forth through nearly endless possibilities)? What determines the way in which a text is to be read (e.g., as a literary figuration of deep themes, a historical reflection of a time and place, a test of one's abilities, a guide for future living, and so on and so forth through nearly endless possibilities)?

The answer to both of these questions is this: Social (really, socio-cultural) groups (families of certain sorts, churches, communities, schools, workplaces, clubs, academic disciplines, interest groups, and so on and so forth through nearly endless possibilities) engage in shared practices using texts. These groups and their practices, how and in history, *make* a text function as a certain type (or genre) and demand that it be read in a certain way (and not others). For the teenage hard rock fan, the lyrics of a heavy metal song are a different type of text read (and consumed) in a different way than the same lyrics are by a cultural studies professor in an avant garde English department. *Dr. Seuss* in the hands of myself and my three-year-old is a different type of text read in a different way than it is in the hands of preschool teachers and students focused on early phonemic awareness. It is different, again, in the hands of an African-American mother and her three-year old focused on the language values of her own culture. As Lucy Calkins points out (Calkins, Montgomery, Santman, with Falk, 1998), one and the same passage is a very different sort of text read in a very different way on a reading test, in "real life," and in various nontest school-based practices.

Learning to read a text of a given type in a given way, then, requires scaffolded socialization into the groups and social practices that make a text of this type to be read in this way. Being able to read a text of a given type a given way requires that one is a member of such social groups and is able to engage in their practices. And here is the final rub: those practices, even as they recruit written texts centrally, rarely involve only written text. They involve ways of talking and listening, acting and interacting, thinking and believing, and feeling and valuing, as well. All this—types of text, ways of reading them, social groups and their practices that go beyond writing—is what falls under the notion of "something" when we talk about reading *something* and have to say what that something is. To leave the *something* off, which is what the Academy's report ultimately does, is to leave out language, learning, development, society, culture, and history. It is, in the end, ironically, to leave out reading.

## Beyond Reading and Language Abilities

Here is where we have gotten thus far: while recent reading reports stress early phonemic awareness, such early phonemic awareness appears to be a side effect of more general "language abilities." Furthermore, what sorts of "language abilities" one gets (and nearly everyone gets lots of different "language abilities" early in life) and how well one is (or is not rewarded) for the sorts of language abilities one brings to school are matters that have to do with issues of race, class, and gender and the workings of culture and politics within and across institutions in our society. What I want to suggest now is that a term like "language abilities" is itself a code for a much broader set of issues.

In today's high-tech, global world, upper-middle-class children who come to school already accelerated for school-based success have had (and continue to have) a plethora of interrelated experiences that far transcend storybook reading (the mainstay of the home-school literature) or reading at all. They have multiple and repeated experiences of diverse texts, media images, videos, computer programs, activities, and experiences (e.g., trips and museums) that allow them to practice (in an integrated fashion) cognitive, language, and social skills that will be richly rewarded at school.

For example, a four-year-old (mine, to take an actual example) may have the video of Disney's *A Bug's Life* movie, *A Bug's Life* CD ROM with games and activities, several different books related to *A Bug's Life* (some stories with pictures, some sticker books, some activity books), other books on bugs more generally (some of them children's books, some adult ones), and a children's bug-collecting kit. The child will switch from one to the other of these, each containing different types and genres of language, activities, and images, related in multiple and diverse ways.

The child's engagement will be scaffolded by different types of adult talk, some of it closely related to academic registers. With the parent, the child repeatedly relates texts to other texts, texts to other symbolic forms (images, oral language, activities), and texts to the world, all the while recruiting many different types of thinking (e.g., narratives, descriptions, and classificatory schemes) and language (e.g., technical names and descriptive phrases encoded in restrictive relative clauses) that are recruited and rewarded later in school. And, yet, all this *A Bug's Life* material is but one of a myriad of such materials, all of them interrelated at a higher level.

All this requires certain sorts of material resources, epistemological and linguistic resources (e.g., adults with allegiances to certain forms of knowing, acting, and talking), and ideological resources (e.g., adults with certain sorts of value-laden orientations to words, deeds, and institutions). This is not meant to imply that families without these resources do not have other sorts of equally good resources. But it is to imply that certain sorts of resources get "cashed out" in terms of mainstream school success and others do not. It is to imply, as well, that these resources go far beyond phonemic awareness, decoding, or even "reading" (in any but the broadest sense).

While it would be instructive to give a description of the whole set of texts, images, activities, and ways of thinking that such a child repeatedly engages with prior to entrance to school (and, of course, afterwards, as well), due to limitations of space, I want to take just one very mundane—almost trivial—example. Through this example (one event of literally thousands like it that occur prior to formal schooling) I want to stress the sorts of "language abilities" that lead to later success in reading at school. Clearly a great deal more than phonemic awareness is involved here (though this child also performs a lot of activities that directly or indirectly build early phonemic awareness). The term "language abilities" is not really right here, either. What is involved is far broader. Perhaps we should use the term "sociocognitive abilities and orientations with respect to diverse school-related semiotic resources," if it were not so cumbersome a phrase.

The event is this: an upper-middle-class, highly educated father approaches his three-year-old (3:10) son who is sitting at the kitchen table. The child is using an activity book in which each page contains a picture with a missing piece. A question is printed under the picture and the space left for the missing piece. The child uses a "magic pen" to rub the space and "magically" uncovers the rest of the picture. The part of the picture that is uncovered is an image that constitutes the answer to the question at the bottom of the page, though, of course, the child must put this answer into words.

In the specific case I want to discuss here, the overt part of the picture was the top half of the bodies of Donald and Daisy Duck. The question printed at the bottom of the page was this: In what are Donald and Daisy riding? (Note the specific register in which this question is written. It is not the more vernacular form: "What are Donald and Daisy riding in?")—the child uses his pen to uncover an old-fashioned Model T sort of car with an open top. Donald and Daisy turn out to be sitting in the car.

The father, seeing the child engaged in this activity, asks him, after he has uncovered the car, to read the question printed below the picture. Notice that the father has not asked the child to give the answer to the question, which is a different activity. The father is confident the child could answer this latter question and has a different purpose here. His purpose is, in fact, to engage in an indirect "reading lesson," though one of a special and specific sort.

The father is aware that the child, while he knows the names of the letters of the alphabet and can recognize many of them in words, cannot decode print. He is also aware that the child has on several previous occasions, in the midst of various literacy-related activities, said that he is "learning to read." However, in yet other activities, at other times, the child has said that he "cannot read" and thereafter seemed more reluctant to engage in his otherwise proactive stance toward texts. This has concerned the father, who values the child's active engagement with texts and the child's belief, expressed in some contexts and not others, that he is not just learning to read, but is, in fact, "a reader."

We might say that the father is operating with a tacit theory (cultural model) that a child's assuming a certain identity ("I am a reader") facilitates the acquisition of that identity and its concomitant skills. In fact, I believe this sort of model is fairly common in certain sorts of families. Parents co-construct an identity with a child (attribute, and get the child to believe in, a certain "competence") before the child can actually fully carry out all the "skills" associated with this identity ("competence before performance"): identity before competence.

So, the father has asked the child "to read" the printed question below the picture of Donald and Daisy Duck sitting in the newly uncovered car. Below, I give the printed version of the question and what the child offered as his "reading" of the question:

Printed version:            In what are Donald and Daisy riding?
Child's reading:            What is Donald and Daisy riding on?

After the child uttered the above sentence, he said: "See, I told you I was learning to read." He seemed to be well aware of the father's purposes. The child, the father, the words, and the book are all here "in sync" to pull off a specific social practice. And this is a form of "instruction," but a form that is typical of what goes on inside socialization processes.

The father and son have taken an activity that is for the child now a virtual genre—namely, uncovering a piece of a picture and on the basis of it answering a question—and incorporated it into different *meta-level activity*. That is, the father and son use the original activity not in and for itself, but as a platform with which to "discuss" reading or, perhaps better put, to co-construct a cultural model of what reading is. The father's question and the son's final response ("See, I told you I was learning to read") clearly indicate that they are seeking to demonstrate to and for each other that the child "can read."

From a developmental point of view, then, what is going on here? First, the child is acquiring, amidst immersion and adult guidance, a piece of a particular *register* or *social language*. The question he has to form—and he very well knows this—has to be a *classificatory question*. It cannot be, for instance, a narrative-based question (e.g., something like "What are Donald and Daisy doing?" or "Where are Donald and Daisy going?"). Classificatory questions (and related syntactic and discourse resources) are a common part of many school-based (and academic) social languages, especially those associated with nonliterary content areas (e.g., the sciences).

The acquisition of this piece of a social language is, in this case, scaffolded by a genre that the child has acquired, namely: uncover a piece of the picture, form a classificatory question to which the picture is an answer (when the parent isn't there to read the question for the child), and give the answer. The genre bears a good deal of similarity to a number of different non-narrative language and action genres (routines) used in the early years of school.

We may note, finally, in regard to social languages, that the child's question is uttered in a more vernacular style than the printed question. So syntactically it is, in one sense, in the wrong "style" (though it is perfectly grammatical from a core grammar perspective, despite what school grammars might say). However, from a discourse perspective (in terms of the function its syntax carried out), it is in just the right style, (i.e., it is a classificatory question). And it is a mainstay of child language development that the acquisition of a function often precedes acquisition of a fully "correct" form (in the sense of "contextually appropriate," not necessarily in the sense of "grammatically correct").

In addition to acquiring a specific piece of certain sorts of social languages, the child is, also, as part and parcel of the activity, acquiring several specific "cultural models" (tactic theories or viewpoints, see Gee, 1999b). One of these is a cultural model about what reading is. The model is something like this: reading is not primarily letter-by-letter decoding, but the proactive production of appropriate styles of language (e.g., here a classificatory question) and their concomitant meanings in conjunction with print. This is a model that the father (at some level quite consciously) wants the child to adopt, both to sustain the child's interest in becoming a "reader" and to counteract the child's claims, in other contexts, that he "can't read."

Of course, the child's claim that he "can't read" in those other contexts reflects that, in other activities, he is acquiring a different cultural model of reading, namely one something like this: reading is primarily the ability to decode letters and words and one is not a reader if meaning is not primarily driven from decoding print. And, as his socialization proceeds, the child will acquire yet other cultural models of reading (or extend and deepen ones already acquired).

The genres, social languages, and cultural models present in this interaction between father and son exist, of course, in conjunction with ways of thinking, valuing, feeling, acting, interacting and in conjunction with various mediating objects (e.g., the book and the "magic pen"), images (the pictures of Donald, Daisy, and the car), sites (kitchen table), and times (morning as father was about to go to work). In and through the social practices which recruit these genres, social language, and cultural models, the three-year-old is acquiring what I call a Discourse with a capital "D" (Gee, 1999b). The father and the child are co-constructing the child as a reader (and, indeed, a person) of *a particular type*, that is, one who takes reading to be the proactive production of appropriate styles of language and meanings in conjunction with print. This socially situated identity involves an orientation to oneself as an active producer (not just consumer) of "appropriate" meanings in conjunction with print, in this case, turn out to be school and academically related.

However, this Discourse is not unrelated to other Discourses that the child is or will be acquiring. I have repeatedly pointed out above how the social language, genre, and cultural models involved in this social practice are in full alignment with some of the social languages, genres, cultural models, and social practices the child will confront in the early years of school (here construing schooling in fairly traditional terms).

At the same time, this engagement between father and child, beyond being a moment in the production of the Discourse of "a certain type of reader," is also a moment in the child's acquisition of what I call his "primary Discourse" (Gee, 1996). The child's primary Discourse is the ways with words, objects, and deeds that are associated with his primary sense of self formed in and through his (most certainly class-based) primary socialization within the family (or other culturally relevant primary socializing group) as a "person like us." In this case, the child is learning that "people like us" are "readers like this."

Now consider what it means that the child's acquisition of the reader Discourse (being-doing a certain type of reader) is simultaneously aligned with (traditional) school-based Discourses and part of his acquisition of his primary Discourse. This ties school-related values, attitudes, and ways with words, at a specific and not some general level, to his *primary sense of self and belonging*. This will almost certainly affect how the child reacts to, and resonates with, school-based ways with words and things.

I would argue that it is these sorts of resources (not just "skills" and "abilities") that must be faced in any discussion of success and failure in early reading in school. It is these sorts of resources that underlie children's success in early reading at school, but also, and more importantly, their success as learners of content and academic identities throughout schooling. We cannot, however, discuss such issues without also discussing issues of identity, class, race, gender, privilege, equity, and access. What upper-middle-class parents create for their children and what elite schools reproduce is a certain "way of being in the world" or "form of life" to which only certain sorts of people have access or allegiance. Children who just learn how to decode, but not how, at the very least, to relate and react to this "form of life" are, in my view, fodder for the "fourth-grade slump."

# References

Aronowitz, S., & DiFazio, W. (1994). *The Jobless Future: Sci-tech and the Dogma of Work*. Minneapolis: University of Minnesota Press.

Berkenkotter, C., & Huckin, T.N., eds. (1994). *Genre Knowledge in Disciplinary Communication: Cognition/Culture/Power*. Norwood, NJ: Lawrence Erlbaum.

Bransford, J.D. & Schwartz, D.L. (1999). "Rethinking Transfer: A Simple Proposal with Multiple Implications." In A. Iran-Nejad & P.D. Pearson, eds., *Review of Research in Education 24*, (pp. 61–100).

Cain, K. (1996). "Story Knowledge And Comprehension Skills." In C. Cornoldi & J. Oakhill (eds.), *Reading Comprehension Difficulties: Processes and Intervention* (pp. 167–192). Mahwah, NJ: Lawrence Erlbaum.

Calkins, L., Montgomery, K., & Santman, D., with Falk, B. (1998). *A Teacher's Guide to Standardized Reading Tests*. Portsmouth, NH: Heinemann.

Carnoy, M., Castells, M., Cohen, S., & Cardoso, F.M. (1993). *The New Global Economy in the Information Age: Reflections on Our Changing World*. University Park, PA: Pennsylvania State University Press.

Chall, J.S., Jacobs, V., & Baldwin, L. (1990*). The Reading Crisis: Why Poor Children Fall Behind*. Cambridge, MA: Harvard University Press.

Chaney, C. (1992). "Language Development, Metalinguistic Skills, And Print Awareness In 3 Year Old Children." *Applied Psycholinguistics* 13(3), (pp. 485–499).

Christie, F., ed. (1990). *Literacy for A Changing World*. Melbourne: Australian Council for Educational Research.

Coles, G. (2000). *Misreading Reading: The Bad Science That Hurts Children*. Portsmouth, NH: Heinemann.

Cope, B., & Kalantzis, M. (eds.). (1993). *The Powers of Literacy: A Genre Approach to Teaching Writing*. Pittsburgh: University of Pittsburgh Press.

Elley, R. (1992). *How in the World Do Students Read?* Hamburg: The Hague International Association for the Evaluation of Educational Achievement.

Ferguson, R.F. (1998). "Teacher's Perceptions and Expectations and the Black-White Test Score Gap." In C. Jencks & M. Phillips (eds.), *The Black-White Test Score Gap* (pp. 273–317). Washington, DC: Brookings Institution Press.

Freedman, A., & Medway, P. (eds.). (1994). *Learning and Teaching Genre*. Portsmouth, NH: Boynton/Cook.

Gee, J.P. (1996). *Social Linguistics and Literacies: Ideology in Discourses*. Second edition. London: Taylor & Francis.

Gee, J.P. (1999a). "Reading and the New Literacy Studies: Reframing the National Academy of Science Report on Reading." *Journal of Literacy Research* 31.3: (pp. 355–374).

Gee, J.P. (1999b). *An Introduction to Discourse Analysis: Theory and Method*. London:

Routledge.

Grissmer, D., Flanagan, A., & Williamson, S. (1998). "Why Did the Black-White Score Gap Narrow in the 1970's and 1980's?," in C. Jencks, & M. Phillips (eds.), *The Black-White Test Score Gap.* Washington, DC: Brookings Institution Press, (pp. 182–226).

Hedges, L.V. & Nowell, A. (1998). "Black-White Test Score Convergence Since 1965," in C. Jencks, & M. Phillips (eds.), *The Black-White Test Score Gap.* Washington, DC: Brookings Institution Press. (pp. 149–181).

Holland, D., Lachicotte, Jr., W., Skinner, D., Cain, C. (1998). *Identity and Agency in Cultural Worlds.* Cambridge, MA: Harvard University Press.

Holland, D., & Quinn, N. (eds.). (1987). *Cultural Models in Language and Thought.* Cambridge: Cambridge University Press.

Jencks, C., & Phillips, M. (eds.). (1998). *The Black-White Test Score Gap.* Washington, DC: Brookings Institution Press. (pp. 401–427).

Labov, W. (1972). *Language in the Inner City.* Philadelphia, PA: University of Pennsylvania Press.

Martin, J.R. (1998). *Factual Writing: Exploring and Challenging Social Reality.* Oxford: Oxford University Press.

Mishel, L., & Teixeira, R.A. (1991). *The Myth of the Coming Labor Shortage: Jobs, Skills, and Incomes of America's Workforce 2000.* Washington, DC: Economic Policy Institute.

National Assessment of Educational Progress. (1997). *NAEP 1996 Trends in Academic Progress.* Washington, DC: U.S. Government Printing Office.

Neisser, U. (ed.). (1998). *The Rising Curve: Long-Term Gains in IQ and Related Measures.* Washington, DC: American Psychological Association.

Scarborough, H.S. (1998). "Early Identification of Children at Risk for Reaching Disabilities: Phonological Awareness and Some Other Promising Predictors." In B.K. Shapiro, P.J. Accardo, & A.J. Capute (eds.), *Specific Reading Disability: A View of the Spectrum.* Timonium, MD: York Press. (pp. 77–121).

Snow, C.E., Burns, M.S., & Griffin, P. (eds.). (1998) *Preventing Reading Difficulties in Young Children.* Washington, DC: National Academy Press.

Steele, C.M. (1992). "Race and the Schooling of Black America." *Atlantic Monthly* (April): (pp. 68–78).

Steele, C.M., & Aronson, J. (1995). "A Threat In The Air: How Stereotypes Shape The Intellectual Identities And Performance Of Women And African Americans," *Journal of Personality and Social Psychology* 69(5), (pp. 797–811).

Steele, C.M., & Aronson, J. (1998). "Stereotype Threat And The Test Performance Of Academically Successful African Americans," in C. Jencks & M. Phillips (eds.), *The Black-White Test Score Gap.* Washington, DC: Brookings Institution Press. (pp. 401–427).

Taylor, D. (1998). *Beginning to Read and the Spin Doctors of Science.* Urbana, IL: National Council of Teachers of English.

Wagner, R.K. (1997). "Phonological Awareness Training and Reading." Paper presented at American Educational Research Association Conference, March, Chicago, IL.

**Chapter Three**

## Reading Research and Skills-Emphasis Instruction: Forging "Facts" to Fit an Explanation

*Gerald Coles*

Let's start with two musical riddles: First, what does it take to get an 85-year-old nun to dance the hokey-pokey? If you guessed that she's been turned-on by a musical version of the New Testament, you're wrong. She is dancing the hokey-pokey because it is part of a musical phonics program she coauthored more than forty years ago and was more recently cited in a national reading report that endorsed "explicit, systematic phonics instruction" as a method that "enhances children's success in learning to read." The nun still teaches the program to kindergartners, and therefore dances to its musical lessons.

Now the second riddle: "What would further enliven this joyous dancing? Answer: A major article on the phonics program and the national reading report in the most widely read national newspaper, *USA Today* (Henry, 2000). "Friends of phonics dance for joy" is the title of the June 5, 2000 article, above which is a large photograph of Sister Marcella Kucia, the 85-year-old nun, dancing with kindergartners while teaching *Plaid Phonics*. Quoted in the article is a representative of the company that publishes the program, who observed that the recently released report of the National Reading Panel (NRP) and its endorsement of phonics "does confirm us." And summing up the joy was the subtitle of the article: "How sweet the sound of endorsement, five decades later."

Before saying more about sounds and symbols, and the NRP report, it is worthwhile adding a word about the sound-symbol connections in the phonics program's title. The name *Plaid Phonics* was "inspired by the pattern on uniforms worn for decades in Catholic schools throughout the USA," but the phonetic irregularity of the word "plaid" seems not to have bothered the authors or publisher of the program. Usually, as all of us who remember the phonics golden rule that when two vowels go walking, the first one does the talking, the sound of the first vowel in "plaid" should be long, as in laid, main, or raisin. When I first read the program's title, remembering the phonics canon, I thought the name of the program was "Played Phonics," not an unreasonable, rule-grounded guess, I think.

The joyful *USA Today* article was only one of many media reports announcing the panel's findings and emphasizing, as *Education Week* (self-described as America's "education newspaper of record") reported: "Reading Panel Urges Phonics For All in K-6" (Manzo, 2000). Although the report urged more than phonics in reading instruction, the media coverage was generally correct because the panel stressed that beginning readers should attain an early mastery of sound-symbol connections, and that this mastery—as well as mastery of other facets of reading—should be taught through explicit, systematic, direct instruction. Implicit in the panel's report and explicit in most media reports was the rejection of a whole language approach to literacy (National Reading Panel [NRP], 2000).

As someone who followed the panel from its inception, I was not surprised by the report's conclusions. The panel was conceived, promoted, and picked by a division of the National Institute of Child Health and Human Development (NICHD) that has, in research, policy, and legislation, championed this form of literacy education (Goodman, 1998; Taylor, 1998). The outcome was also predictable because, as I will explain below, the majority of the panel had considerable publications and public materials that revealed they shared reading theories and instructional views with those who selected them.

Before discussing the panel members, however, a brief overview of some of the history leading up to the panel's creation is necessary. Plans to create this panel followed other attempts to establish that explicit, systematic, direct reading instruction that emphasizes early mastery of skills had solid scientific evidence supporting it. Many advocates of this form of instruction had hoped that it would obtain an official stamp of approval with the 1998 National Academy of Science report, *Preventing Reading Difficulties in Young Children* (Snow, Burns, Griffin, 1998). However, despite the long support given by many members on the *Preventing Reading Difficulties* committee to skills-first instruction, the contrary views of a few members forced a modicum of compromise. As a result, portions of the report could be interpreted as recommending a "balanced" approach that made teachers responsible for determining the extent and method of skills instruction. Whether the totality of the report could be read this way is a matter I will not examine here; suffice it to say, given the various individual and organizational interpretations of the report, it surely provided less than a firm endorsement of the skills-emphasis views of the reading research division of NICHD.

Shortly after *Preventing Reading Difficulties* was released, the NICHD, an organization with considerable Congressional support of its views on reading, especially among conservative Republicans, obtained a Congressional "request" that it organize a study of "the effectiveness of various approaches to teaching children how to read" and report the "best ways to apply these findings in classrooms and at home" (NICHD, 1998). Describing it as a "request" is like saying that Boeing got a "request" from the Pentagon to build bombers. That is, that the company chair and board, by merely overseeing the manufacturing work—and without ever lobbying, making campaign contributions, and sitting in chairs that revolve between the company board and the Pentagon—received the request in the mail one fine day.

Although the Department of Education was formally included as a consulting organization in this undertaking, the NICHD spearheaded the selection, organization, and administrative processes of the panel for this study. All information about the panel flowed from the NICHD, and Duane Alexander, Director of the NICHD, was the chief spokesperson in all information releases. When the panel members were announced, Alexander was the only person on the "selection committee" who was quoted in the press release.

As I indicated above, the panel was slanted toward the NICHD direct, explicit, systematic instruction of skills view of the best way to teach, the best way to learn, the best kind of classrooms, the best kind of training programs, the best reading materials, the best way to explain the causes of reading problems, the best way to understand the reading process, the best kind of research, and the best way to be a researcher. Nevertheless, Alexander praised the "diversity" of the panel (Manzo, 1998).

The extent of this diversity can be discerned in the following overview of the fourteen panelists. One was a major NICHD researcher, a recipient of considerable NICHD funding, and a leading member of an NICHD-supported university research site. There was no question what "review of the literature" she would encourage and conclusions she would reach. There might have been little objection to her participation had she been part of a genuinely broad representation of views—if, for example, a researcher with an opposing position had also been on the panel, one who might have publicly and consistently criticized the NICHD perspective commensurate with the NICHD supporter. But there was no such person. One panel member was a school principal with a whole language orientation, but she did not have the research background for the close review of dense, detailed, and often abstruse empirical research required of the panel in a relatively short time.

Another panelist was active in various literacy groups at the state and local levels in Texas, and in Governor George W. Bush's Reading Initiative Task Force. One of these groups strongly promoted skills-emphasis direct instruction in beginning reading and had, in fact, invited

NICHD-supported researchers to speak to local teachers. Should this kind of activist have been on such a panel? The answer could have been "Yes" had the panel consisted of genuine broad representation.

The research and publications of a third panelist contained an interpretation of reading development fully in accord with that in the NICHD research. For him, sight reading of words and knowing the connections between spelling and sounds were foundational in beginning reading instruction.

A fourth panelist was editor of a journal that had devoted an entire issue to NICHD reading research. Guest editors of the special issue were two NICHD-supported reading researchers. With respect to "diversity," we can again ask, "Did the panel include an editor of an educational journal with an alternative viewpoint?" Once more, the answer is "no."

The work of yet another panelist was based on very narrow models of information processing (e.g., how orthographic information, such as phonemic, visual, and letter-order information affects comprehension). This panelist's research on reading disabilities, like that of NICHD reading research, identified phonological awareness problems as key in causing the disabilities. Both the sixth and seventh panelists had done considerable work on a model of the reading process that corresponded with the one predominant in NICHD research. Without question, these seven panelists had a published record of views on reading indisputably comparable to those held in the NICHD.

The views of the remaining panelists were not as invariably similar to those of the NICHD. One panelist had written extensive assessments of reading research that suggested he might serve as a broker for contending sides, but a close look at his publications indicated that he would most likely consider the direct instruction of skills to be a scientifically validated teaching approach and would accept a report that did not include a full appraisal of opposing teaching approaches.

The ninth panelist had publications sympathetic to views contrary to those in the NICHD research, and might have been expected to be the least partisan among the reading experts. Nonetheless, given the instructional inclination of the panel, the extent to which this member would actively dissent from the majority opinion was not clear.

Two additional panelists were educators, but not reading educators. One had worked in early childhood development and had done research on social competency and self-concept development in kindergarten programs. Another had done work on gender influences in the classroom, and on race and ethnic relations. These two could have been expected to be impartial, but impartiality for anyone not familiar with the scholarship in an academic field is dependent, first and foremost, on having a full representation of views before them, and that full representation depended on the panel's reading researchers providing it.

The same could be said of the chair of the panel, the Chancellor of the University System of Maryland, and a physicist by profession. He was said to have the "ability to forge consensus on difficult issues," but how could he have done so if the panel's reading researchers did not provide all sides of the "difficult issues" ?

The thirteenth panelist was a reading teacher in the Houston, Texas, schools, where prominent NICHD research had been done. There was no biographical information disclosing her views on reading education, and I could find no publications she has authored.

Only one panelist, a principal and former teacher, had a clear affiliation with whole language. This panelist had written a guide for developing a whole language program in schools and articles on literacy improvement generally sympathetic to a whole language orientation. Perhaps the inclusion of this panelist was what Alexander had in mind when he spoke about "diversity."

In addition to the instructional direction in which the reading researchers leaned, most, if not all, of their research was quantitative and empirical, containing a limited, narrow focus on variables that influenced learning outcomes the kind of research that the NICHD advocated and funded. There was no representation of qualitative research, ethnographic research, critical literacy research, research on influences "external" to the classroom that shape teaching and learning, whole language research, sociohistorical research, social process research, or other kinds of research approaches and assumptions about the nature of reading and learning to read.

## What Was The Result?

The researchers' primary method of evaluating research was a meta-analysis of studies they identified as scientifically sound and which they examined to appraise the relationships between instructional methods and reading achievement outcomes. A meta-analysis accomplishes this by taking a group of studies that have examined these relationships and averaging their statistical calculations that estimate the effect of the methods on achievement. The average in the meta-analysis is termed the "effect size." As the NRP explained, the effect size was the statistic that measured "the extent to which performance of the treatment group exceeded performance of the control group" (NRP, pp. 2–3). An effect size of 1.0 revealed "a strong" instructional effect, and an effect size of 0 indicated that the instructional method had no effect. An effect size of .50 would indicate a moderate effect.

The report concluded that the direct, explicit, and systematic instruction of skills provides the foundation for reading and the prerequisites for comprehension. Teaching children phonemic awareness, the panel advised, "was highly effective under a variety of teaching conditions with a variety of learners across a range of grade and age levels" because it "significantly improves their reading more than instruction that lacks any attention" to phonemic awareness (NRP, Summary, 2000, p. 7). "Systematic phonics instruction" too, stated the panel, "produces significant benefits for students in kindergarten through 6th grade and for children having difficulty learning to read" (NRP, Summary, 2000, p. 9).

Although the report has been described as one that recommends a combination of methods, the extent to which that "combination" is skewed toward an emphasis on word skills can be discerned by a word count of the concepts and aspects of reading that was included in the NICHD press release announcing the report. Counting the words in both the title and the body of the press release, the term "comprehension" was mentioned seven times and "thinking," zero times, compared to skills terms (phonics, phonemic awareness, phonemes, and sounds), which collectively were mentioned twenty-nine times.

If we look at the units of language emphasized in the press release, we find that "word" or "words" was mentioned nine times compared to the complete absence of any larger units of languages, such as "sentence," "paragraph," "story," or "book." Overall, the press release reflected the report and the media portrayal of the report: one reigning method stood head and shoulders above the competition.

## How Valid Are The Report's Conclusions?

The NRP report, it has been said, offered a seemingly independent, objective appraisal of the NICHD brand of education, one that could promote skills-emphasis beginning reading instruction across the nation. In Connecticut, for example, the "major findings" of the report were cited as one of the chief pieces of evidence for a state teaching guide on the "ingredients essential to the most basic mission of school: teaching a child to read" (Green, 2000). Although the Connecticut Associate Commissioner of Education stated that the teaching guide advocated both "explicit teaching of the nuts and bolts and comprehension," like the NRP report, the state teaching guide recommended less than a balanced combination of methods. As a reporter observed, "those of a certain age will recognize" that "the [guide] is heavy on what some might see as old-fashioned: spelling, vocabulary building, the importance of punctuation, practicing the sounds that make up words." And when Reid Lyon, chief of the NICHD division of reading research, was asked about the state teaching guide, he replied, "The research is telling us what is critically important—that kids need to know how to read. What people have finally realized is that no child will be able to access that unless they have the nuts and bolts." Summing up her appraisal of the reading research, Louise Spear-Swerling, a contributor to the state teaching guide, concluded that there is little debate now about how to teach reading: "There is a tremendous amount that we know about how children learn to read. If we apply this, it can make a huge difference" (Green, 2000).

In my previous writings (Coles, 1998, 2000) I have analyzed the empirical research on teaching the "nuts and bolts" of reading and concluded that the studies fell far short of supporting claims that they validate this form of instruction. In the following pages I want to examine the NRP's reiteration of these claims and discuss why the report fails to justify "nuts and bolts" teaching.

A problem with the meta-analysis approach that the panel used is that it confines itself to input and output information provided in the studies and is not a vehicle for a detailed examination of the studies themselves that can reveal their deficiencies, strengths, reasoning, definitions, characteristics of teaching and learning, and other critical aspects in any study on literacy instruction. Therefore, not only can a meta-analysis not be better than the quality of the studies it pools together, it can also be misleading if it ignores an appraisal of these crucial qualities. Fortunately, although the panel used a meta-analysis as its chief mode of analysis, it did provide some detailed interpretations of a number of studies, thereby enabling us to gain some insight into the panel's methods, reasoning, and objectivity in reviewing the research. Because of space limitations, I will discuss five studies described and interpreted in the first section of the NRP report, studies which I have previously reviewed in detail (Coles, 1998, 2000).

## Causation Versus Correlation

The report states that a study by Share and colleagues (1984) "showed that PA was the top predictor along with letter knowledge" of later reading achievement and that "PA correlated [positively] with reading achievement scores in kindergarten [and with] scores in 1st grade" (NRP, 2000, pp. 2–11). Unfortunately, the report does not discuss the meaning of the term "predictor." And even if the meaning itself was not controversial, does the term mean that a factor that predicts something is a cause of it? Not necessarily, as Share and colleagues themselves note, but the NRP panel omits quoting this caveat, and instead, in its interpretation of the study, implies an equivalence between "predictor" and causality.

The panel's failure to probe the question of causality is especially evident in its lack of discussion of the third strongest predictor of reading achievement found in the study, that is, success on a "finger localization" test (one in which a child whose vision is blocked identifies which of her or his fingers an adult has touched). Despite its predictive correlation with future reading achievement, finger localization skill in itself could not be considered "causal" to learning to read, and no educator would suggest finger location training as a beginning reading method.

The report also fails to discuss what the researchers themselves said about their finding that letter knowledge was a strong predictor of future reading. Did its predictive strength mean that beginning readers needed to know letter names in order to get off to a fast, secure start in reading? For Share and colleagues the answer was "no." They point out that although "knowledge of letter names has been traditionally considered the single best predictor of reading achievement . . . there appears to be no evidence that letter-name knowledge facilitates reading acquisition" (p. 1313). Again, correlation does not necessarily equal causation. Letter name knowledge is likely to represent experience and accomplishments with early written language that are part of, and contribute to, literacy attainment; the knowledge can be considered to be a "marker" of these experiences and accomplishments (Coles, 1998, ch. 3). None of these issues are captured in the NRP report's simplistic summary that the study "showed that PA was the top predictor along with letter knowledge." This study, like many other investigations of phonological awareness, identifies predictors that are in fact "products" related to a variety of experiences with written language.

## The Missing Control Group

A striking example of how the panel's interpretation of the research accords with its prior conclusions about reading is the report's discussion of a 1997 study by Brennan and Ireson [NRP, 2000 pp. 2–35]. The report states that a "PA treatment group" was "compared to one no-treatment group" and the "effect size was impressive." This provides evidence, says the panel, that the "Danish program [later translated into English and coauthored by Marilyn Adams and Barbara Foorman] "can be used effectively in American classrooms" (NRP, 2000, pp. 2–35; Adams & Foorman, 1998).

The comparison that the report made was correct as far as it went, but what the NRP report did not tell readers is that there were, in fact, two control groups, not one. Besides the one described by the panel—the no-treatment group—another control group learned phonological awareness in an informal, "as needed" way similar to the way skills are taught in a whole language approach. In other words, what we have in this study is an opportunity to compare children learning PA either through a training program or an implicit, "as needed" method. Although this comparison would have provided the panel with an opportunity to delve into the question of how PA should be taught and learned, it chose not to take advantage of this opportunity.

Let us do so. At the end of the school year the phonological awareness training group did significantly better on phonological tests, but there were "no significant differences between the [training and implicit teaching] groups on the rhyme and syllable synthesis tests or on the tests of word reading and spelling" (Brennan & Ireson, 1997, p. 251). The panel's report noted only the phonological test results and omitted all the others, (those in which there were no significant differences). The researchers who did the study observed, moreover, that "the significantly superior scores achieved by the training group in this study on tasks of phonemic awareness suggest that this group should also achieve higher scores on the reading tasks, but this was not in fact the case" (p. 257). Again, the conclusions were not quoted in the NRP report.

The researchers went on to propose that the "writing experiences" of the informal learning group might have accounted for their reading success. On average they "wrote longer stories than either" the training group or the normal kindergarten group (p. 258). These conclusions too were omitted from the NRP report.

In other words, the study showed that in order for children to learn rhyme, syllable synthesis, word reading, and spelling, they do not require such a training program. Furthermore, extensive writing activities are likely to be effective for attaining the literacy knowledge for which the researchers tested. The training group did do better on PA test tasks because those were the kind of tasks on which the program focused. However, this research offered no evidence of the superiority of PA training transferring to measures of reading ability.

Moreover, this study lends some support to a holistic written language approach insofar as it indicates that phonological skills can be readily learned within a rich array of reading and writing activities. It also demonstrates that there not only is no need for a stepwise approach to literacy learning, such an approach can reduce time spent on essential and productive literacy activities, such as "writing experiences."

## Training Compared to What?

Benita Blachman and her colleagues (1994) conducted a study in which low-income, inner-city kindergartners were taught phonemic awareness and letter-sound correspondence, and were compared with a control group that followed "a traditional kindergarten curriculum that included instruction in letter names and sounds" (NRP, 2000, pp. 2–35). According to the NRP report, the "results of the study were very positive" because the "children receiving PA training outperformed controls on PA tasks" and the "training transferred to reading ([effect size:] 0.65) and to spelling (0.94)." (NRP, 2000, pp. 2–35).

A problem with both this study and the NRP interpretation of it is that neither deal with the issue of "training compared to what?" Because the control group had only minimal written language activities (learning letters and their sounds), it is impossible to conclude from this study that phonemic awareness and grapheme-phoneme correspondence training is necessary for kindergartners. What can be said following the study is that kindergartners engaged in PA training were helped in learning to read more than were children who engaged in learning letters and their sounds, which, as discussed above in the study by Share and colleagues, reading researchers have not found to be significantly beneficial as a beginning reading activity. No other conclusions can be drawn because the training program was not compared to another approach to written language development. The study certainly does not demonstrate that PA training is necessarily the written language experience that will have the best impact on kindergartners' future reading development.

## PA Training and Real Classrooms

Another example of how the NRP report, in its mustering of "evidence" for the superiority of PA training, ignored the issue of "training compared to what?" is a study by Joanna Williams (1980). The NRP report described the study as one in which students ages seven to twelve were taught to "segment and blend phonemes first in speech and then using letters" (2000, pp. 2–35). Later work involved phonics exercises in decoding words and learning to spell the sounds in words. At the end of the training period, the NRP report states, the training had a significantly superior effect in decoding words and nonwords compared to "the untreated controls." For the NRP this demonstrated that the program "was highly effective at teaching decoding skills to disabled readers" (2000, pp. 2–36).

Omitted from the NRP report is any information about the students and the instructional curriculum, information the panel apparently did not consider relevant in appraising "effect size." The Williams' paper itself explains that the children were identified as "learning disabled" and in special education classrooms in New York City (in schools in Harlem and the Lower East Side). She states that "the regular reading instruction [in 1975] provided in these classrooms might best be described as eclectic. Teachers used a different basal reading program in almost every classroom; only one series was used by three teachers, and two other series were used by two teachers each. About 75% of the teachers also used phonics materials. (Sometimes the phonic component of the basal series and sometimes a separate phonics program was used.)" (p. 8). Worksheets too were part of the curriculum.

What we have, in other words, are special education classes that appear to be doing nothing "special" with the students. No doubt the classes were going through the basal readers at a slower pace, but there is no indication that the classrooms used anything other than the traditional, conventional reading programs used in the regular classes, reading programs that perhaps were those that contributed to the students' reading failure in the first place.

Therefore, we could say that the phonemic awareness and phonics programs were helpful as an adjunct to a conventional basal reading program used in conventional special education classes in 1975, classes that duplicated at a slower pace the literacy program that the children used before being placed in special education. This is not a persuasive demonstration of the "effect size" of PA training or the need for such training over alternative approaches. Again, both the meta-analysis and the panel's portrayal of the study ignored critical qualities of the instruction examined in the study.

## Direct or Indirect Teaching of Skills

The NRP also called attention to a study by Iversen and Tunmer (1993) because, said the report, it demonstrates that adding phonological awareness training to a Reading Recovery program could increase the speed with which children completed the program (NRP, 2000, pp. 2–39). In this study, two forms of Reading Recovery were compared, a "standard" approach and another that included explicit phonological awareness teaching. In the standard approach, once children could identify at least 35 of the 52 alphabet letters (upper and lower forms), the portion of time devoted to learning the letters was replaced by additional storybook reading in which word analysis activities, such as phonological awareness, were learned incidentally within the reading activity. In the modified program, this time was devoted to direct teaching of phonological awareness. Children learned sounds at the beginning, middle, and end of words; sounds added, deleted, and substituted in words, etc.

The NRP report acknowledged that "both groups performed" similarly "on PA outcomes and reading outcomes" at the end of the training period and at the end of the school year. Nonetheless, the NRP report emphasized, the children in the modified group "attained prescribed levels more quickly than children receiving the standard program," thereby demonstrating that "adding PA training improved RR by increasing its efficiency" (pp. 2–39).

Let us look closer at this "efficiency."

The modified Reading Recovery group ended its work in 8.5 weeks, the standard group in 11.5 weeks. Although this three-week difference might be significant for school budgets, for example, lost on the panel was the demonstration in the study that, in fact, phonological skills need *not* be taught *directly* because they can be learned as part of a program that emphasizes reading as a "whole" activity. Furthermore, the finding that both groups were essentially at the same achievement level at the end of the first year does not necessarily mean that the instruction in which children learned "more quickly" was the better one and the study itself did not investigate any other meanings in this time difference. Important educational questions needed to be addressed, such as, "What literacy benefits might accrue from a program that gave relatively greater emphasis to reading storybooks?" If an intervention program were extended for a few weeks, and the students could engage in other kinds of literacy experiences, what additional gains might the students also make?

## Sidestepping the "Simple Theory"

The NRP described another study as one that added PA training to a Reading Recovery program (Hatcher, Hulme, & Ellis, 1994) and showed that "effect sizes, though small, favored the PA-training group" for reading and spelling (pp. 2–40). Here, the researchers compared three combinations of phonological training and reading instruction. One group, the "phonology training alone," used a program that taught word segmentation, rhyming words, sound synthesis into words, and similar phonological tasks.

A second group, called "reading with phonology," used the training program taught to group one, but also devoted time to reading and rereading books, writing stories, and engaging in phonological activities related to the stories. The reading program used a Reading Recovery model (reading and rereading books, writing stories, etc.) but, as the researchers stated, the study made "several changes" in the way the "teaching strategies and diagnostic tests" of the model were presented (p. 47).

At the completion of the study, the "phonology training alone" group had finished the entire program, whereas "the reading with phonology" group finished approximately half of it.

A third group, a "reading alone" group, used a contorted model of Reading Recovery. That is, the students did writing and reading activities similar to those of the second group, but, unlike the Reading Recovery method  or virtually anything resembling good teaching!—the teacher omitted "any explicit reference to phonology" or letter-sound relationships regardless of children's needs or desires. Hence we see one glaring misrepresentation in the NRP report: in fact, no "Reading Recovery" program was compared to other groups using PA training programs. Approximately one year after the various forms of instruction were completed, the groups were compared and the "reading with phonology" group was found to have statistically superior test results in reading comprehension, word identification, and spelling. (Note that this group completed *half* the phonological activities.)

How do these results compare to the NRP version?

It is important to point out first that the researchers undertook to examine the prevailing "simple theory that there is a direct causal path from phonological skills to reading skills."   For example, Marilyn

Adams, Barbara Foorman, and their colleagues (1998), in the introduction to their phonemic awareness training program manual, state, "a child's level of phonemic awareness on entering school is widely held to be the strongest single determinant of the success that she or he will experience in learning to read or, conversely, the likelihood that she or he will fail" (p. 2).

Upon completion of their experiment, however, the researchers concluded that "phonological training alone is not a powerful way of improving children's reading skills." Although the "phonology training alone" group "made significantly more progress in phonological skills than" the other groups, this superiority did not translate into comparably superior literacy test scores. Consequently, they proposed that their findings "cast doubt on the simple theory that there is a direct causal path from phonological skills to reading skills" (pp. 52–53). In other words, the study shows that phonological training alone is not sufficient for creating the "causal" agent that phonological awareness has been claimed to be, an important conclusion omitted from the NRP report.

Does the study show that effect sizes "favored the PA-trained group," as the NRP report explains (2000, pp. 2–40)? No. Not only does the report omit the researchers' own conclusions about the "causal" role of phonological awareness in learning to read, it also fails to discuss the bizarre "reading alone" group, with its potentially damaging teaching method hopefully not found in any actual classroom. The inclusion of this group simply demonstrates that teaching that forbids paying any attention to skills regardless of children's needs or desires is poor teaching. It is hardly a foil demonstrating the superior "effect sizes" of the "PA-trained group."

## Experts Opinions and Appraisals of Scientific Evidence

These are just a few examples of the extensive misrepresentation of the empirical evidence that fills the NRP report. More documentation of this misrepresentation can be found in my critical reviews of other studies contained in the NRP report (Coles, 1998, 2000). Yet despite the report's failure to provide the scientific evidence for the instruction it advocates, it remains largely unchallenged and is being used as a gold standard to justify legislative and policy mandates for rigid, direct, skills-emphasis beginning reading instruction across the nation.

The slanted representation of views on the panel can be found in other panels charged with reviewing scientific issues. For example, physician and cancer expert Samuel Epstein has written about the skewed direction of scientific panels asked to review cancer research. A concern about cancer issues prompted the president of the National Academy of Sciences and a dozen other presidents of national science academies to create "an International Academy Council as a global science advisory board" that would provide "impartial scientific advice" to governments and international organizations (Epstein, 2000). Epstein's analysis is especially pertinent to issues of objectivity in reviews of literacy research because the National Academy of Sciences (NAS) and its suborganization and think tank, the National Research Council (NRC), provided the vehicle and publishing house for the influential *Preventing Reading Difficulties* (Snow, Burns, & Griffin, 1998), issued prior to the NRP report.

Assessing the advisory board's impartiality, Epstein concluded that the NCR's committee that issued a 1996 report on carcinogens in the human diet "trivialized concerns on cancer risks to infants and children from food contaminated with carcinogenic pesticides." Acting on behalf of a coalition of experts in public health and cancer prevention, Epstein described the advisory board as "grossly unbalanced and disproportionately weighted with industry consultants." These conflicts of interests were not unique, Epstein emphasized. The NCR's "biotechnology panel" in 1999 was composed of experts who were part of a "revolving-door relationship between the industry and National Research Council" (Epstein, 2000).

## Science and Education

The misuse of science I have reviewed here and more extensively elsewhere, should not feed cynicism that scientific evidence is simply in the eyes of the beholder and can play no objective role in informing and improving teaching and learning. Science can and should play this role, but can only do so within certain conditions. Foremost among these conditions and at the outset is a clear determination of educational goals and the kind of education we want for children.

Addressing the role of science in education, John Dewey posed the following question: What "intellectual guidance to the practical operating of schools" can science, understood as "a body of verified facts and tested principles," provide? (Dewey, 1959, p. 116). Answering the question, Dewey cautioned that nowhere more than in education is it "more dangerous to set up a rigid orthodoxy, a standardized set of beliefs to be accepted by all"—nowhere more than in education is the "claim to be strictly scientific more likely to suffer from pretense" (p. 116).

In other words, the horse race science that has been increasingly cited to justify one form of instruction over another contains a set of beliefs about educational outcomes. Because the educational approaches have different views of what education should be, science provides only information and insights that will be limited to what is considered useful to differing approaches. There is no way out of this unless, Dewey jested, "society and hence schools have reached a dead monotonous uniformity of practice and aim." As long as there is no uniformity in either society or schools, "there cannot be one single science" (p. 116). Because progressive education differs from traditional education by definition and practice, its scientific aims and research are also different.

This is not to say, Dewey emphasized, that there is a sharp divide between instructional approaches on each and every issue. One could "occasionally borrow" from the science of another when it is relevant to its "special aims and processes." But Dewey stressed that borrowing was "a very different thing from assuming that the methods and results obtained under traditional scholastic conditions form the standard of science to which progressive schools must conform" (p. 117).

Unfortunately, nearly a century after this was written, we are still a long way from understanding and applying these insights. Teachers are asked to accept a model in which scientists sit on high, appraise research, and then hand down to policymakers and publishers scientific findings on the "best way to teach literacy." The policymakers, in turn, transform these scientific findings into policy while the publishers transform the findings into scripted, teaching materials. Beneath these tiers patiently stand the teachers, who reach up to accept and then apply the policy and materials in their classrooms. To topple this model, teachers will have to fight for an alternative educational vision, an undertaking which will, from the outset, require understanding and countering the pseudoscience that has been damaging literacy teaching and learning, bamboozling many teachers and much of the public, and, regrettably, thwarting the valuable role science could play in helping to advance educational knowledge and practice.

# References

Adams, M., Foorman, B. (1998). *Phonemic Awareness in Young Children: A Classroom Curriculum.* Baltimore: Paul H. Brookes.

Blachman, B., (1994). Kindergarten Teachers Develop Phoneme Awareness in Low-Income, Inner-City Classrooms, *Reading and Writing* 6, (pp. 1–18).

Brennan, F., & Ireson, J. (1997). Training Phonological Awareness: A Study to Evaluate the Effects of a Program of Metalinguistic Games in Kindergarten, *Reading and Writing* 9, (pp. 241–263).

Coles, G. (2000). *Misreading Reading: The Bad Science That Hurts Children.* Portsmouth, N.H.: Heinemann.

Coles, G. (1998). *Reading Lessons: The Debate Over Literacy.* N.Y.: Hill & Wang.

Dewey, J. (1959). Progressive Education and the Science of Education, in *Dewey on Education: Selections*, ed. M. S. Dworkin. N.Y.: Teachers College Press, (pp. 113–126).

Epstein, S.S. (May 12, 2000). The Cancer Prevention Coalition Charges National Academy of Sciences With Proposing Secret World Science Court. Press Release. (www.preventcancer.com/PRS/May 12,00.html/) .

Goodman, K. (1998). Comments on the Reading Excellence Act. *Reading Online* (www.readingonline.org).

Green, R. (September 8, 2000). A New Recipe for Reading Education. *Hartford Courant.* (www.ctnow.com).

Hatcher, P.J., Hulme, C., & Ellis, A.W. (1994). Ameliorating Early Reading Failure by Integrating the Teaching of Reading and Phonological Skills: The Phonological Linkage Hypothesis, *Child Development* 65. (pp. 41–57).

Henry, T. (June 5, 2000). Friends of Phonics Dance for Joy: How Sweet the Sound of Endorsement, Five Decades Later. *USA Today.* (p. D6).

Iverson, S, & Tunmer, W.E. (1993). Phonological Processing Skills and the Reading Recovery Program. *Journal of Educational Psychology* 85. (pp. 112–126).

Manzo, K. (April 8, 1998). NICHD Chief Names Closely Watched Panel on Reading Research. *Education Week.* (p. 24).

Manzo, K. (April 19, 2000). Reading Panel Urges Phonics For All in K-6. *Education Week.* (pp. 1–14).

National Institute of Child Health and Human Development (NICHD). (March 27, 1998). Panel to Assess New Readiness of Reading Research for Use in Nation's Classrooms. Press Release.

National Reading Panel. (2000). *Teaching Children to Read: An Evidence-Based Assessment of the Scientific Research Literature on Reading and Its Implications for Reading Instruction.* Washington, D.C.: NICHD.

National Reading Panel Summary. (2000). *Teaching Children to Read: An Evidence-Based Assessment of the Scientific Research Literature on Reading and Its*

*Implications for Reading Instruction.* Washington, D.C.: NICHD.

Share, D. L., et. al. (1984). Sources of Individual Differences in Reading Acquisition. *Journal of Educational Psychology* 76. (pp. 1309–1324).

Snow, C., M. Burns, S., & Griffin, P., eds. (1998). *Preventing Reading Difficulties in Young Children.* Washington, D.C.: National Academy Press.

Taylor, D. (1998). *Beginning to Read and the Spin Doctors of Science.* Urbana, IL: National Council of Teachers of English.

Williams, J.P. (1980). Teaching Decoding With an Emphasis on Phoneme Analysis and Phoneme Blending." *Journal of Educational Psychology* 72. (pp. 1–15).

# Chapter Four

## Literacy Packages in Practice:
## Constructing Academic Disadvantage

*Patricia D. Irvine*
*Joanne Larson*

In this chapter, we will describe our study of elementary teachers piloting a commodified literacy package in an urban district serving pre-dominantly low-income African-American and Latino students. The focus of this chapter is on teachers' perceptions of the reading series and their use of the materials in pedagogical practices. In the district we studied, the central administration had piloted several new literacy packages to choose one for the entire district. The administration believed that adopting a single series would improve students' low reading achievement scores by standardizing instruction and retraining those teachers suspected of having marginal skills. However, interviews with teachers participating in the pilot and observations of their classroom practices showed that teachers used the materials selectively, choosing activities to remedy what they perceived as students' deficits in oral language and academic abilities. We will present data from our study of this pilot to show that the autonomous definition of literacy (Street, 1995) that underlies the materials, in combination with a deficit model of students and their linguistic and cultural resources, resulted in pedagogical practices that academically disadvantage the students whom the district is trying to serve.

We define commodified literacy materials as those materials produced by profit-oriented publishing corporations. Included in this definition are basal reading programs and their associated instructional materials. Packaged literacy materials have been criticized for the limited view of literacy they promote and because they attempt to script teachers' behaviors, deskilling them in the process (Apple, 1990; Beyer, 1988; Goodman, Shannon, Freeman, & Murphy, 1988; Luke, 1988; Shannon, 1992). Our study adds to the literature critical of commodified materials by suggesting that it is not just the materials themselves, but how they are used in practice that influences literacy education. Moreover, we suggest that commercial materials, as key components in literacy events (Heath, 1983) and literacy practices (Street, 1995), are imbricated in a nexus of social practices in local contexts that are linked to broader cultural and political practices (Barton, Hamilton, & Ivanic, 2000). In this study, we observed how commercial materials were used to reinforce teachers beliefs about deficit views of students and, in effect, to construct student disadvantage in the classroom use of the materials.

In the first part of the chapter, we will define the autonomous model of literacy (Street, 1995) that underlies the reading series we studied in use and that informs the practices of the teachers we observed. We contrast it with the ideological, or social practice, approach to literacy that we use to interpret the results of the study. Then, we will describe the qualitative study we conducted of a literacy package used in one urban district. In our discussion of the findings, we argue for more empirical research on the use of commercial materials in local contexts that also accounts for the social, political, and historical factors affecting their use. We close the chapter with suggestions for educators who must prepare preservice teachers to enter schools mandating the use of commercial materials.

## Autonomous and Ideological Models of Literacy

The commercial materials we observed in use are based on an approach to literacy that can be characterized as autonomous (Street, 1995). Street contrasts autonomous approaches to literacy with ideological ones to focus attention on the role of social context in reading and writing, teaching and learning literacy, and in researching these practices.

In the autonomous model, literacy is represented as the sum of the parts of written language, such as letter-sound correspondence and phonemic awareness, and learning to read is a matter of acquiring technical decoding skills that are presumed to operate independently of context (cf., Snow, Burns, & Griffin, 1998). Autonomous approaches to literacy have warranted the description of "scientific" literacy universals, or decontextualized skills that are assumed to govern the processes of reading and writing across contexts (Shannon, 1992). However, as Edelsky (1994) writes, "The activity of performing divisible sub-skills may have little or no relation to the indivisible activity we call reading" (p. 115). Although it is possible to break written language down into a structuralist system of interrelated linguistic subparts, the analysis into parts does not provide a blueprint for how people learn to read; learning to read entails more than acquiring these so-called building blocks of text in sequential order. In Street's definition of literacy as ideological (1995), the cognitive processing of linguistic parts is wholly dependent on context because it takes place "within cultural wholes and within structures of power" (Street, 1995, p. 161).

An ideological view of literacy assumes that literacy is a set of social practices that are historically situated, highly dependent on shared cultural understandings, and inextricably linked to power relations in any setting. In a social practice framework, social and linguistic practices are mutually constituted within past and present power relations among people who write and read to accomplish social goals. In this model, the context is constituted by local, culturally specific practices that circumscribe who has access to learning to read and write which kinds of texts for which purposes. Individual differences may affect the process, but only within the constraints and possibilities afforded by the cultural, historical context.

While approaches to literacy based in an autonomous model assume that literacy is context-free, an ideological approach seeks to understand how literacy forms and practices have evolved to serve culturally specific purposes. Street (1995) presents ethnographic sketches of literacy in a variety of international settings and at different historical periods to emphasize the deeply contextual nature of literacy practices. For example, he describes how school-based literacy, i.e., forms of literacy that are valued in schools, is culturally produced and rooted in essayist textual practices of Western academic elites. This autonomous definition of literacy grounds the literacy package being studied in this district. Street (1995) argues that through the "pedagogization" of literacy, autonomous, objectified conceptions of literacy are naturalized in practice and, as we argue here, reified in literacy packages. The notion of pedagogization captures the socially constructed link between institu-tionalized processes of teaching, learning, and literacy.

If all forms of literacy are thus socially constructed in context to meet the social needs of readers and writers, then what students construe to be legitimate practices and uses of literacy are mediated by the social relations that constitute instruction (Luke, 1988). In a social practice approach, students learning literacy would have opportunities to use reading and writing to access the world, not as objects of instruction, but as the subjects of meaning-making (Coles, 1998; Edelsky, 1991; Freire & Macedo, 1987). However, in settings dominated by skills-based pedagogies, students are constrained in what they are enabled to do with and through text. In this study, teachers interpreted and used the commercial materials to support reading pedagogies that denied students a role in the coconstruction of social meaning.

We draw on Street's ideological view of literacy to analyze the classroom practices we observed in this study and to situate them in the social and institutional contexts in which they occur (Bloome, 1987; de Castell & Luke, 1986; Edelsky, 1991; Graff, 1987; Irvine & Elsasser, 1988; Scribner & Cole, 1981). In an ideological model, macro social and political factors, such as who has access to the middle-class social and cultural resources that schooling values and promotes, are understood to profoundly influence what happens in the micro context of the literacy classroom. Thus, the teachers we interviewed who hold deficit views of their African-American students' oral language abilities do so within an institutional and historical context that validates these beliefs. Attitudes toward the use of nonstandard languages in schooling are institutionalized, formally and informally, in local and national language education policies. In this study, those macro social attitudes manifest themselves in teachers' beliefs about students' language abilities and their pedagogical decisions based on these beliefs. Commodified literacy materials grounded in autonomous definitions of literacy preclude the recognition of students' language as valid cultural resources. Students are then offered few opportunities to participate actively in the construction of textual, cultural, or social meaning—to learn to read, in other words.

## Context of the Study

The data are drawn from a larger study of an urban school district's reading reform process. Northeast City School District is a medium-sized urban district whose current central concern is raising test scores for its more than 37,000 students. In recent years the test scores of several city schools, both elementary and secondary, were so low that the State Department of Education considered placing the schools on its list of low performing schools. Only 72 percent of third graders passed the standardized achievement tests in reading in the year prior to this study. By contrast, in suburban schools the reading scores are dramatically higher: the range of scores is 99 percent to 86 percent, with a median score of 97 percent; in Northeast City School District, 80 percent of the students are non-White (African-American, 60 percent; Latino, 18 percent; and other, 2 percent) while 79 percent of the teachers are White (see Figure 1).

**Figure 1: Racial/Ethnic Breakdown in Northeast City School District by Percentage**

| Racial/Ethnic Background | Students | Teachers | Administrators |
|---|---|---|---|
| African-American | 60% | 15.5% | 31.1% |

**Figure 1:  (continued)  Racial/Ethnic Breakdown in Northeast City
School District by Percentage**

| | | | |
|---|---|---|---|
| White | 20% | 79% | 61.5% |
| Latino | 18% | 4.6% | 6.6% |
| Asian/Pacific Islander, Native American, East Indian, or other. | 2% | 9% | .8% |

Total K-12 enrollment:    37,153
Full time staff:              5,298

The textbook reform process examined in this study reflects one of
this district's responses to accountability mandates from the State
Department of Education. In addition, city government was pressuring
the district to address the downward spiral of achievement scores
because it seemed to be driving families seeking better schools out of the
city to neighboring suburbs. In response to these pressures, district
administration mounted a reading reform effort that began with piloting
three new textbook series, one of which would be selected for district-
wide implementation the following year.

The administration claimed that one reason for low reading scores
was the discontinuity of reading pedagogy in a district with high student
mobility. In the previous ten years, four separate series and the packaged
phonics drill program, Open Court Reading (1995), had been adopted in
various parts of the district. Some teachers echoed administrators'
concerns, suggesting that a single, mandated reading series would
provide consistency in instruction, particularly for those students who
move frequently within the district. In the interview segment below, one
teacher, after describing how 50 percent of her students moved in one
year, expressed her desire that the district decide on one series.

Excerpt 1:
    That's one of the reasons we need, if you bring anything back (to the
District) we need one program throughout because each program. . . . it's
crucial in this District. Every program teaches letters in a different sequence. If
we were all on the same program . . . (it would be more consistent).

The administration also hoped a new textbook series would improve
reading instruction by teachers they considered to be only marginally
qualified. One district official believed that all the teachers should be re-
credentialed, stating that she wished they could "start over" with new

teachers who were better trained. Administrators hoped that by mandating the use of a new textbook series, instruction would be scripted and, as a result, the quality of instruction would be guaranteed. Teachers in the pilot and administrators all believed that the new reading series would teach reading (Shannon, 1992).

While the administration had already decided to adopt a new textbook, they had not determined how to evaluate the pilot. District administration asked Larson to assist in the evaluation of the textbook pilot by observing and interviewing selected teachers. This observational component was only one part of a larger evaluation that included surveys of teachers, parents, and administrators.


## Study Design and Methodology

A qualitative design was used to seek the teachers' beliefs about reading instruction, their perceptions of the materials, and their use of the materials in practice. In this study of eight inner-city schools, nine teachers were observed (seven White and two African-American), both male and female, in grade levels kindergarten through third grade. Principals selected highly regarded teachers to pilot the textbook series. The pilot teachers received a letter and consent form asking them to participate in the observational component of the pilot process. The nine teachers who participated in this study were the only ones who responded to the letters. District administrators were careful to establish that Larson was not hired by the district and, therefore, outside the official textbook adoption process. The classrooms represented a range of sociodemographics based on the percentage of students on free-and-reduced lunch (43-100 percent), student mobility indicators, and reading achievement scores (ranging across the nine classrooms from 93 percent to 56 percent, with a median score of 76 percent).

Using ethnographic methods, the teachers were observed twice during the project to document how they used the textbook series. Fieldnotes were taken during each observation. Interviews were conducted and audiotaped following each observation and were transcribed to analyze teachers' beliefs about the teaching of reading, their perceptions of the materials, and their patterns of textbook use. Several additional teachers who declined to be observed were interviewed by telephone and each conversation was documented in fieldnotes.

Some teachers declined to participate, stating that they were uncomfortable being observed, that they had not received letters of consent until too late, or that they thought the decision had already been made by the district. As reasons for not participating, several teachers alluded indirectly to being over-committed in their schools or to the ongoing union and contract dispute. Textbook publishers and their representatives appear to have contributed to some of the teachers' confusion. For example, pilot teachers received an abundance of extra resource materials from textbook representatives in what seemed to be an attempt to sway their decisions. This created mixed feelings about the textbook adoption process among some teachers, as they believed that the district would not be able to purchase all the materials they had been given. In some pilot schools, publishers also gave manuals and associated supplies to teachers not piloting any series. One publisher even attempted to contact Larson to solicit advance information on the findings of this study.

The following research questions guided this study: What factors do teachers believe contribute to learning to read? How do the teachers in the pilot perceive the commercial packages? How do they use the materials in their instructional practices? The database consists of twenty-four hours of audiotaped interviews and full transcriptions of tapes along with comprehensive fieldnotes of all classroom observations. Two observers (Larson & Pope, 1997) conducted several observations in each classroom. Larson and Irvine (1999) coded the data separately to establish patterns and relationships, then agreed upon a set of categories for analysis. Using the constant comparative method of analysis (Glaser & Strauss, 1967; Strauss & Corbin, 1990), a link emerged between teachers' beliefs about students' lack of language abilities and how they used the series and associated materials.

## Findings from the Study

**What Factors Do Teachers Believe Contribute to Learning to Read?**
In interviews, teachers stated that in order to read, students need appropriate background experiences and oral language ability. They were unabashed about expressing their deficit views of students (Hull, Rose, Fraser, & Castellano, 1991), attributing reading difficulties to students' home environments and lack of middle-class background experience. They also cited students' lack of oral language and lack of parental involvement as reasons for poor reading scores. Teachers in the study believed that their students enter their classrooms at an insurmountable

deficit. In the following excerpt, one first-grade teacher described her students as coming to school "in a hole":

Excerpt 2:
    Learning to read is so complicated. If they can come to first grade knowing letters and knowing some sounds, having been read to, they'll be ready to learn to read. I do not get many children like that in here. They do not come to kindergarten ready for kindergarten. So I'm always looking at children who aren't ready to learn yet. And that's a sad fact. But it's true. Nevertheless, you have to keep on truckin'. They come in, *in the hole,* that you have to dig them out of. That's not a very easy thing to do. I know that people downtown will tell you that it can be done. I'm here to tell you it can't be done.

She believed that her students were not ready to learn when they came to school and that no matter what "downtown" (i.e., district administration) said, she could not bring the students to grade level. Another teacher, referring to what she believed "our population" needed, stated the following:

Excerpt 3:
    I think that's something you just have to be diligent about, especially in terms of our population that doesn't have a lot of exposure to stories outside of classroom necessarily. Many students do not know any letters of the alphabet when they come to school at all. It's almost like a foreign language to them.

This view of students as entering school at a deficit was a common belief, whether the teacher was White or African-American. This teacher's comment seems to reference the kinds of skills that middle-class children often come to school already knowing (Heath, 1983). Similarly, the African-American first-grade teacher in the following excerpt focuses on the importance of appropriate background experience as the main contributing factor to students learning to read:

Excerpt 4:
    Background experience is the main factor. How much they've been read to. Whether they've been to the zoo, to the museums. What experiences they bring. Because, I always say I need to write these things down cause I forget, but it's strange how simple things that you just think, "Oh, 6, 7, years old, they know what this is." And then you mention it and no one has any idea what you're talking about. You know? (chuckle) So background experience plays a big part.

The appropriate background experience she refers to is one that middle-class children may take for granted. According to Heath (1983), middle-class language socialization is the model for school-based literacy practices, so poor and working-class children who come without them must learn them in school. As we will suggest later in this chapter, students without middle-class backgrounds are unlikely to learn those skills when instruction is based on materials and practices grounded in autonomous definitions of literacy.

In addition to identifying students' lack of appropriate background experience as contributing to their reading difficulties, all the teachers felt that their students' reading difficulties stemmed from a lack of oral language. To some teachers this meant Standard English, while others seemed to suggest that students lacked the ability for natural language:

Excerpt 5:
I think the first thing we have to do is that we have to give them the language, help them develop language, not just vocabulary but speaking in sentences, hearing ... very good examples of language through literature.

Another third-grade teacher with twenty-five years of teaching experience offered the following:

Excerpt 6:
Sometimes I wonder if these children are used to hearing correctly spoken English for any sounds.

The teacher used the term "these children" to refer to the fifteen students in his classroom, fourteen of whom were African-American. Indirect references to this district's student population of predominantly African-American students were common across the data. "Our (or this) population," "inner city kids," and "urban students" were terms both White and African-American teachers used consistently to refer to children in their classrooms. In the excerpt below, a first-grade teacher elaborates:

Excerpt 7:
I think ESL should be in every classroom. I think it's teaching of language practices. I think that all little ones need to learn how to speak. And I think here in the city we have students who come in and [are] even further behind with their ability for language and speaking in full sentences.

Her utterance, "here in the city" refers to her perception that city school district students come in so underprepared for language learning that they need to be taught English as a Second Language (ESL) to catch up to the immigrant children in the district who are nonnative speakers of English.

All teachers in the study perceived students' social class and language as deficits, overlooking the cultural and linguistic resources that students do bring to school. The deficit model has been deeply critiqued since the publication of Bereiter and Engelman (1966), who offered an instructional model for teaching "disadvantaged" children not unlike the practices we observed in this study. They argued that African-American children show ". . . very close to the total lack of ability to use language as a device for acquiring and processing information. Language for them is unwieldy and not very useful" (1966, p. 39), a stance uncomfortably close to the statements of many teachers in this study. As the next section shows, teachers' perceptions of what their students needed to overcome these deficits drove their pedagogical decisions and their selection of activities from the reading series.

## How Do Teachers Use The Packaged Materials In Instructional Practice?

The commercial reading series presented an elaborate script for teachers to follow, and teachers were under surveillance by the district for close adherence to the textbook and the manual. At the same time, district personnel advised teachers to base their selection of activities on students' needs. In classroom observations, teachers selected some activities and ignored others, relying heavily on their previous practices. In interviews, they explained how they selected activities from the series to meet the perceived needs of their students.

All teachers stated that there were far too many suggested activities in the teacher's manual to possibly accomplish in the suggested time or in the time they had for language arts instruction. Teachers at all levels of experience expressed the tension they felt between the district expectations that they "really do the pilot" and the need to "pick and choose" among the plethora of activities. "Covering everything" or "getting it all in" within a certain time period emerged as a major concern of both experienced and inexperienced teachers.

> Excerpt 8:
> There are so many ideas in these manuals that if I did everything, we would never come close. We're not I do not know if we're going to come close, anyway to completing (chuckle) but I wouldn't, I probably, I'd be only half way to where I am now if I did everything in the manual. There's so much to choose from. *And all of it is good.*

This teacher, like others in the study, did not question the content, scope, or sequence in any of the piloted series. They generally accepted that all activities were appropriate and represented good pedagogy. The overwhelming criticism of any series was that there were so many ideas that it was difficult to choose. Because there were so many suggested activities, teachers were forced to "pick and choose":

Excerpt 9:
   It's very difficult to squeeze in the pieces and next year if this were the series chosen I would *pick and choose* a little bit differently. You would see a little bit less than was suggested I do today.

The experienced teachers were concerned that beginning teachers might find the textbook series manual too full of ideas and lack the experience to judge what could be eliminated or what was essential. One teacher with more than ten years, experience stated the following:

Excerpt 10:
   Once you get used to looking at manuals, I mean after time, you've taught for a while, you really may not even need a manual ... I think that it's probably user friendly and I think that ... it has lots of activities. The problem is that it probably has too much. And I think that sometimes it would be hard for a beginning teacher to pick and choose what's most—appropriate? Or most meaningful.

Under pressure to complete the list of activities, some teachers omitted optimal teaching practices that they had previously used with the district's encouragement, such as learning centers, collaborative projects, writer's circle and others, even similar practices suggested as supplementary in this literature-based textbook series. For example, during field observations, teachers commented that learning centers were something they rarely had time for anymore. It is important to note that institutional constraints, such as special events, assemblies, and outside classes (physical education or art) also took time away from the two-and-one-half hour daily language arts period that the district mandates for language arts. A number of teachers made creative use of resource teachers, assistants, and volunteers to gain as much time as possible for a main "lesson." Resource teachers, aides, and volunteers were observed conducting teacher-constructed drills or overseeing students identified as needing special education services on specific tasks.

In the following excerpt, the teacher refers to using the textbook for practice, extension, and reteaching activities, all of which emerge from an autonomous view of literacy as an accumulation of decontextualized skills. Furthermore, she expresses her appreciation that activities were already thought out, saving her the time and trouble of doing it herself:

Excerpt 11:
   I think there's so much to do that I would have to spend 2 or 3 weeks on every story to get every activity done. And when they did

introduce the reading series to us they told us that it's not designed to do every single activity that they outline in it, but it's to think of the needs of your children. And I really think that works out really well that way. It gives you so many different things to choose from. It's an excellent resource and it's helped save me time for having to think up activities on my own and what I like to do is I'll use their ideas for practice activities or extension activities or reteaching in class and the workbook pages I'll use for the review.

This teacher was observed in instruction to choose extension activities and workbook pages that focused on reading subskills. Teachers in this study, under time pressure and forced to choose among an abundance of suggested activities, selected language arts activities that were discrete and aimed not at the comprehension of whole texts but at developing subskills. As the next section shows, teachers also justified their selection of activities by referring to deficit perceptions of the oral language abilities of this student population.

### *Teachers chose activities based on deficit perceptions of students' needs.*

Teachers consistently referred to their students' need for "pieces of language" and "phonics" to remedy their lack of language ability. In classroom observations of the teachers piloting the textbook series, reading pedagogy was restricted to the teaching of passive decoding skills in which the students were asked to recite someone else's thinking (Nystrand, 1997). Even though the series was literature-based, teachers chose skills-only activities that focused almost exclusively on the word level as a unit of study, with most activities breaking down words into letters and sounds. We observed the following activities in all classrooms: fill-in-the-blank grammar worksheets, phonics drills, spelling tests, vocabulary tests, adjective worksheets, writing prompt exercises, handwriting exercises, letter-sound recognition drills, story sequencing worksheets, character clusters, consonant-cluster and letter-blend drills, alphabetizing, sight-word memorizing, repetition of words and sounds (both oral and written), and whole-class reading exercises. Some of the materials were taken from the textbook series and some were materials the teachers had always used.

We observed no activities during the study in which students read whole texts or participated in activities other than worksheet exercises. Instead, students were engaged in activities that could be termed "doing reading," meaning that they were practicing isolated skills devoid of meaningful context. Students were learning phonemic awareness, letter-sound recognition, and consonant clusters as discrete activities. What counted as literacy in this context, then, was performance on skills exercises (Edelsky, 1991; Routman, 1996). Students were learning isolated skills that were presented in the textbook, but there was no instruction in which this learning came together into meaningful activity that led to reading or writing.

Teachers understood teaching literacy as delivering a set of technical skills as efficiently as possible, explicitly linking the skills they taught to their perceptions of students' abilities. One male third-grade teacher explained it this way:

Excerpt 12:

Um, (2 sec) phonics, I believe, if you, phonics are necessary probably for I'd say 70—80 percent of the kids. 70—80 percent of the kids could learn how to sound out words and how to read through phonics. The remainder of the kids um they use the whole language just straight reading ... Uh, sight words, I think is important. And, um, syllables, breaking, uh, words into pieces so that they may sound out the words a little bit easier. So I'd say, I'd say, say the basics are pretty much taught with basics. I mean break, break everything down in its smallest, simplest form.

In this teacher's classroom, those students who have access to literacy as meaning-making in interaction with text are the 20 percent of students who can do "just straight reading." The majority of the students, however, learn that what counts as literacy are the pieces the teacher has determined are the basics: sight words, syllables, and phonics, with the primary pedagogy being to "break everything down in its smallest, simplest form." The textbook series did not disrupt the autonomous model of literacy that he describes in this excerpt or his beliefs that this model is especially appropriate for this group of students.

Phonics-only approaches were clearly evident in all the classrooms. Given the dominant belief that learning to read follows prescribed stages of development (e.g., from oral to written language), phonics was understood to be an essential first step. What we observed in lessons, however, was that other "steps" did not follow. Instruction remained at the level of basic skills and did not extend to more contextual activities in which students used these strategies to read.

Teachers who felt that their students did not come to school "ready to learn" or with adequate skills in oral language (or Standard English) supplemented the textbook with reading activities they had developed over the years. All the practices observed were grounded in an autonomous model of literacy. Teachers' preferences for using their own previous practices and their judgments about students' limited capabilities governed their selection of activities from the manual and the extent to which they adhered to textbook series recommendations:

Excerpt 13:
  Other things are things that I just have always done …I like doing those
type of activities because it makes them focus more on … the … spellings
…you know, of the word and try to really sound things out. And for them it's
like a game so they enjoy doing it. So that's something I've always done that is
not in the manual. My strategies were basically the same. And that's why I like
the program. You know, I still use the same things now, even with the pilot. I
like the pilot because it seems to fall right in line with the things that I've done
for years.

The majority of teachers in the study supplemented the series with
materials from the four programs mentioned earlier that were in place
prior to the textbook pilot. Several pilot teachers stated that they have
used Open Court exclusively for years to teach reading. For the most
part, none of these teachers planned to alter this practice. One first-grade
teacher explained it this way:

Excerpt 14:
  We're doing . . . Open Court as well. I do not know if you're all that
familiar with Open Court, but you see the cards up there and I do not know if
(series publisher's name) would approve that because it's not really a pure
pilot, but, I'm doing it because it works. So I'm not going to abandon it . . . I
was just afraid to abandon Open Court … Because I've been successful with it.
And I do not know if … Maybe if I just did any kind of phonics everyday, that
would be the same thing. But because I have … the cards, and the do-this-
today, play-the-tape, now-do-this I'm locked into doing it and it's a discipline
for me to do it everyday. Maybe it's more training the teacher than it is the
student.

This teacher, noting that the structure of the series had the effect of
training teachers, echoed the district's hope that a reading series would
retrain teachers and standardize instruction. She admits, however, that
she will not abandon her previous instructional package, based on skills,
in spite of the district's mandate.
  In the following excerpt, an African-American first-grade teacher
explained her use of phonics:

Excerpt 15:
  The manual has so many different activities for you to choose from, um,
my thing is getting them to understand phonics and how we use phonics to
figure out a word. … I tend to rely on phonics. I mean that's—I think phonics
is extremely important. And so, my lessons, the phonics, you know, kind of
guides me. So I always make sure that at some point during the day that we
really, that there is a focus, focus on phonics. And then again, my thing is
always looking at, unfortunately, believe it or not, standardized tests? And you

want to have the kids prepared so you need to make sure that. So, doing what
we did today, with the words in context, kind of trains them you know, for that.
But of course your teacher (refers to a beginner), may not realize until they've
taught three or four or five years or so that they say, "Hey, my kids really need
this so that when it's time for us to really sit down and take the test." I mean
remembering the rules, things like that.

In spite of the many suggestions in the manual, this teacher, like
many others we interviewed, chose not to use them in favor of her own
teaching strategies. In other words, teachers used strategies from the
textbook only when they matched their existing practices. The teacher
cited above enacted her belief that phonics must come first during our
observation of her language arts lesson. She frequently reminded
students about phonics rules, "One does the walking while the other does
the talking," even when the lesson had shifted from language arts into
other content areas. Her language arts lesson consisted of students going
over words from an upcoming story (call, say, eat, fish, to) in which
students were asked to repeat each word, then use it in a sentence. The
lesson followed a strict IRE (initiation, response, evaluation) lesson
format where students responded to test-like questions to which the
answer was already known (Gutierrez, 1993; Mehan, 1979; Nystrand,
1997).

In the next section we bring together interview and observation data
from two classrooms to illustrate what happens when the teachers merge,
in instructional practice, deficit beliefs about students' language and an
autonomous model of literacy.

## Teaching Reading Behaviors, Not Reading

Limiting students' participation in literacy events to performing reading
and writing exercises amounts to asking students to complete a set of
clerical tasks that lead to a formulaic understanding of text (Nystrand,
1997). In classroom observations, teachers in the pilot were observed to
focus primarily on word-sound correspondence drills and reading
behaviors, such as following along in the text, instead of activities in
which students actively interpreted text or made meaning of it orally or
in writing. A first-grade teacher expressed her belief that students were
only capable of completing tasks such as these, but they were not able to
"read":

Excerpt 16:
    What I try to do is make sure we read the story every day and make sure I

do a lot with the vocabulary and the spelling. The comprehension part of it—
they usually do not have a big problem understanding the stories and assessing
the stories, um, it's just the reading of the stories that they, you know. At the
beginning, when they first start learning how to read, you know, just the
attacking the words is the biggest problem.

As we will show in excerpt 17, in this classroom reading consisted of
a whole class read-aloud taken from the piloted reading series in which
students were required to all read together without deviation. The teacher
focused on reading behaviors rather than the word attack or
comprehension strategies she described in the excerpt above. Moreover,
students did not read the story themselves. The teacher read to them as
they followed along, an activity that was not suggested in the teacher's
manual. They comprehended the text based on her oral recitation, but
were not given the opportunity to interpret the text for themselves. In
essence, they cannot read the story because the teacher does not let them.

During the observation of this classroom, children attempting to read
forward to see what was happening in the story were sometimes literally
and physically stopped to concentrate on sounds, explicitly told to finger
one word at a time in unison:

| | |
|---|---|
| Excerpt 17: | |
| Teacher: | We're going to start from the first row. |
| | I want to hear everyone. |
| | Keep your finger on the word. |
| | I want to see you. |
| All: | An egg is an egg until it hatches (reading) |
| Teacher: | What's that word? |
| | Look at the blend. |
| | Third row only. |
| | Where is your finger? |
| | Okay. |
| | Paris, we're still in the book even if you're not reading. |
| | Loud voice in the second row, leader. |
| | Not too fast, |
| | Juan you have to read with everyone else. |
| | Finger under the A. |
| | First row, ready, begin. |
| All: | A block is a block until its a tower (reading). |
| Teacher: | Finger under the A. |
| | Second row, ready, begin. |
| | We need– |
| | Juan, you're interrupting. |
| | You've got the right page. Very good. |
| | You have to read together. |
| | Turn the page. |
| | You're right, the first word is "Nothing". |
| | First row, what's the first word on the page. |
| | Nothing. Okay. |

> Guillermo, you still have to follow.
> (even though it isn't his row's turn).
> You need to turn when I say turn and then you won't be
> confused.

Students were vigilantly monitored to make sure they were reading at the same pace. The teacher asked a series of questions ("What's that word?" "Where is your finger?" "What's the first word on the page?") yet allowed no time for students to answer. In fact, the students did not attempt a response because they knew that the teacher already had the answer (Nystrand, 1997). Except for the oral recitation of text, students had no turn in the discussion. The teacher focused exclusively on teaching "proper" reading behaviors, such as using fingers as pointers, rather than teaching reading strategies that helped students engage students with text.

After this reading period, students were dismissed to their desks to complete a matching worksheet that was not connected to the story but was part of the reading series accessory materials. The teacher read the instructions, then slowly and painstakingly went over each line to make sure they not only had the correct answers, but the same answers completed at the same time. One student secretly traced her finger over the paper where the answers would be on sections that the teacher had not yet reached. She knew not to move at her own pace with her pencil, so she shielded her finger as she answered the upcoming questions on her own.

## Constructing Academic Disadvantage

In the following interview,[1] the teacher described what she termed a verb conjugation lesson that she would conduct later in her classroom. She has taught for five years and has had this particular group of students two years in a row, from second to third grade. On this particular day she had twenty-three students in class, seventeen who were African-American and six who were White. In our interview, the teacher reported the following:

> Excerpt 18:
>     This [lesson] is a conjugation of the verb "be" which is an interesting idea
> in itself considering all the Ebonics (laughter) controversy of things. Because I

---

[1] The following discussion is taken in part from Larson & Irvine (1999). "*We call him Dr. King*": Reciprocal distancing in urban classrooms. *Language Arts*, 76(5), 393–400.

have kids that won't conjugate. I mean they'll use wrong conjugations, ya know, they'll say "he is" or "we is" so this should be interesting today (heh heh) because it's not —it's not natural for some of them to conjugate. So it will be interesting, ya know, to get them to use the correct conjugations of the verb "be."

From this teacher's perspective, the students' language, Ebonics, was the reason for their incorrect or "wrong conjugations" ("he is" or "we is"). The students were, in fact, conjugating verbs, but in their own language, African American Vernacular English (AAVE). Beliefs about students' lack of "natural" language ability are reflective of social and institutional beliefs about nonstandard language, and such beliefs, as we will show, may have negative consequences for literacy learning when put into practice. This teacher's beliefs about her students' language abilities influenced her decision to limit her lesson to a grammar worksheet, as the following observation demonstrates.

The lesson began with the teacher at the front of the room using an overhead projector. She was filling in a worksheet taken from the textbook series. She spoke to the students briefly about singular and plural verbs and began the worksheet exercise by reading the first example, "A horse is stuck." The answer was already filled in on the transparency. She read the next sentence, saying the word "blank" where the answer should have been, then called on students to fill in the answer:

| Excerpt 19: | |
|---|---|
| Teacher: | A horse is stuck. |
| | The horses *blank* stuck. |
| | [Calls on African-American student.] |
| Af. -Am. Student: | The horses is stuck. |
| White Student: | Horses are stuck. |
| Teacher: | We didn't say "horse are stuck." |
| | [To African-American students.] |
| | Would you say "I is hungry?" |
| | Do we say "We is hungry?" |
| | No! |
| Af.-Am. Students: | I do, I do. |
| Teacher: | But you're not supposed to! |
| Af.-Am. Student: | I say "I is going." |
| Teacher: | But you're not supposed to say |
| | [reaches for an example in the manual] |
| | I is (going). |
| | There are words that sound right, |
| | and there are words that are right with these |
| | subjects, and you just have to learn them. |
| Af.-Am. Student: | I was hungry. |
| Af.-Am. Student: | No. I say, I hungry [laughs]. |
| | [Laughter from his classmates.] |

| Teacher: | I'm going to wait a minute . . . |
| | control! [All stop talking.] |
| | Star Wars! |
| | Is there a star up there for Group 1? |
| | Take it down. |
| Teacher: | Molasses cookies *blank*—is or are—Peter's favorite? |
| | What would you say? |
| | [Four or five African-American children say "is" from |
| | different parts of the room.] |

In this example, this teacher's beliefs about her students' inability to make verbs agree with their subjects in Standard English were enacted in a practice that excluded students' language resources as valid in the making of meaning about this text. She positioned African-American students as outside ("we/you") the Standard-English-speaking community. In this literacy event, a social distancing process (Larson & Irvine, 1999) was initiated when she asked questions that elicited what she considered "wrong" answers from African-American students ("Would you say, 'I is hungry'?"). When a student answered with an expression that is correct in AAVE, "No. I say, I hungry," eliciting laughter from his classmates, the teacher then implemented the classroom disciplinary system called Star Wars.

While the fill-in-the-blank exercise observed in this classroom is problematic as a tool for reading instruction because it is rooted in the autonomous model of literacy, it may not be the most academically disadvantaging aspect of this lesson. The teacher's deficit beliefs about language, combined with an autonomous definition of literacy, in effect deny the students access to meaning—making through their own language and literacy practices. A pedagogy based on a ideological definition of literacy would value students as legitimate resources in reading instruction, perhaps not even using the worksheet (see Gatto, this volume) or have used it in a way that assisted students in understanding the grammar of their own language. Students who learn to distinguish the grammatical differences between Standard English and AAVE are better prepared for the school-based literacy they will encounter throughout their education (Christensen, 2000; Elsasser & Irvine, 1985; Perry & Delpit, 1997).

As discussed earlier, we draw on a multidisciplinary perspective to define reading, like literacy, as a social practice in which meaning is constructed in the interaction between teachers, students, and text (Baynham, 1995; Bloome & Bailey, 1992; Cazden, 1992; Gutierrez, Baquedano-Lopez, & Turner, 1997; Luke, 1994; New London Group, 1996; Nystrand, 1997; Street, 1995). What we observed in this study is the social practice of reading in this context. If, as Rogoff (1994) argues, students learn through daily participation in all culturally organized activities and it is only the content that changes, then in the literacy events we observed, they are learning a relationship to text in which they are positioned as consumers of a static body of skills. They are not learning a relationship to text in which meaning is an active construction and interpretation where students are the subjects of meaning-making. Students also learn that they are not members of the institutionally legitimized community, that their language and abilities are not adequate, that knowledge resides in the teacher and the packaged materials, and that what counts as reading and as knowledge belong to the teacher and the institution. Furthermore, students are learning what teachers and texts define as proper reading behaviors rather than reading strategies that will lead to meaning-making and achievement in school-based literacy.

## Conclusion

To districts in search of a quick-fix approach to low reading achievement, a commercial reading series may seem to be a panacea. Publishers promise a curriculum designed by experts and based on a "scientific," autonomous approach to literacy practices, and district administrators are tempted by the prospect of standardizing instruction, "teacher-proofing" the curriculum, in effect. However, observations of these materials in practice—in this district, at least—show that a literacy package neither standardized the reading curriculum nor trained teachers to be better at reading instruction. The commercial materials in this study offered a script and a variety of activities, not all of them skills-based, but teachers only followed parts of it. They interpreted suggested activities in light of deficit ideologies about students' lack of background experience and oral language while continuing previous practices, many of which they derived from other commercial materials.

The findings from this study corroborate the critiques of packaged materials that show them to promote modes of instruction grounded in autonomous models of literacy (Luke, 1988; Shannon, 1992). At the same time, studying packaged materials as they are used in practice complicates our understanding of their impact on students, teachers, and literacy education. In this context, teacher ideologies about students' social class and about literacy learning turned out to be the key determinants in how they selected activities from the packaged series.

Commodified packages may support particularly disadvantaging pedagogies in districts serving primarily poor, working-class, and language minority students. Rist's (2000) research, carried out in 1970 but unfortunately relevant today, shows how poor children in one kindergarten classroom were systematically excluded from participation in higher-level reading and writing activities. Strickland (1994), too, argues that skills-based instruction targeted at children of color tends to foster low-level uniformity and subvert academic potential, and in this study, we observed students being apprenticed to skills-based literacy practices and reading behaviors.

To succeed in school, students in the classrooms we observed need access to different kinds of literacy practices. Knobel's (1999) research on the multiple literacies of children from different social backgrounds suggests that middle-class children often practice more sophisticated literacy skills at home than they do at school by having access to computer technology, for example. Her research shows that working-class students also possess viable community-based literacies, but their resources are often ignored or disparaged. Therefore, given the structural inequalities that limit poor children's access to middle-class literacies in nonschool settings, school may be the only place some children can learn the literacy necessary for school achievement.

In this sense, the packages and practices accompanying them are particularly disadvantaging for the students we observed. The deficit perceptions that teachers hold are reified by the commercial materials and the practices supported by them because students do not, in the end, learn to read in ways that teachers hope or that promote success in school. When teachers implement even more skills practice, a spiral of disadvantage continues.

Although we have focused much of this chapter on critiquing teachers' pedagogical practices using packaged literacy, it is not our intention to blame teachers as individuals. Focusing on individuals obscures the larger institutional and social contexts that not only validate, but impose, the use of commodified materials and the autonomous literacy practices they support. Teachers forced to use the materials (and other packaged series before these) do so in a social and political context, and as the following teacher acknowledges:

Excerpt 20:
    Oh God, no. I've had enough of the district and their policies. And do this and do that. And the testing and everything else. If they decide to develop one reading text for the whole district, I'm kind of stubborn. That'll probably just influence me more not to use it. So I do not care what they [say] ... different kids, different standards.

This teacher's deficit ideology is expressed through her phrase, "different kids, different standards." She means that she does not plan to have the same standards for students she believes are unable to meet them. According to her statement, it is doubtful that the implementation of a packaged series is going to interrupt this ideology. Moreover, she raises the key issue of testing and accountability, key reasons for the district's mandate. This district stands to benefit politically from implementing what appears to be a standardized literacy delivery system. The district can demonstrate accountability to constituents at the local and state levels by committing funds and considerable personnel resources to a colorful, slick, commodified literacy package which promises to raise reading achievement scores. If materials, devised by "experts," cannot help teachers raise student reading scores, then the blame falls back on the students, their families, or the teachers. A district may be able to insulate itself from criticism with the exorbitant purchase of a package, a process noted by Shannon (1992).

Standardized tests are a key tool in this political process, especially if they measure competence in the skills promoted by the materials. Luke (1988) writes that some of the packaged instructional techniques may not necessarily be bad pedagogy, but the assessments that accompany these systems are tautological: They provide their own justification and confirm it in the form of test scores.

In Luke's (1988) review of the development of standardized literacy programs that began in the 1940s and 1950s, he anticipates several key findings from the study we report in this chapter. He describes the implementation of standardized systems as forms of control exercised by state education departments that essentially deskill teachers and then re-skill them in particular ways. He speculates about the double-bind that postwar teachers may have experienced: The texts provided standardized, "scientifically" sanctioned scripts for instruction, but they were also enjoined to be spontaneous and innovative in adapting activities to local needs. However, doing both is not possible, especially given the constraints of frequent standardized testing and accountability measures. In the study we described, teachers' responses to this double-bind were to rely on previous instructional practices, which some teachers said they had learned from other literacy packages. The district's insistence on teachers adhering to a packaged literacy program may, in effect, undermine their goal of helping teachers teach reading better.

As teacher educators, we try to interrupt one small part of this process that we can control, and that is arming new teachers with a theoretical understanding of the differences between autonomous and ideological approaches to literacy (Street, 1995). We structure our teacher preparation course syllabi so that preservice teachers learn how to identify the theoretical underpinnings of any materials they encounter. However, we are still seeking ways to support new teachers as they face institutional pressures to adopt commercial packages. We are developing formal venues, such as grant-funded activities, to make both new and experienced teachers aware of the presence of deficit ideologies in seemingly innocuous teaching methods. In meetings where these issues are explored, experienced teachers are key members of a team we assembled to offer pedagogical alternatives. Informally, we support new teachers who feel isolated by putting them in touch with a vibrant network of excellent teachers who are willing to talk and work with them, teachers who have been able to resist adopting deficit ideologies and who can talk about how they work in contexts with mandated materials. We are seeking more strategies—formal, informal, and political—which can help new and experienced teachers resist district pressures and packaged activities which systematically ignore students' linguistic and cultural resources.

# References

Apple, M. (1990). *Ideology And Curriculum*. New York: Routledge.

Barton, H., Hamilton, M. & Ivanic, R. (2000*). Situated Literacies: Reading and Writing in Context*. London: Routledge.

Baynham, M. (1995). *Literacy Practices: Investigating Literacy In Social Contexts*. New York: Longman.

Bereiter, C., & Engelman. (1966). *Teaching Disadvantaged Children in the Preschool*. Englewood Cliffs, NJ: Prentice Hall.

Beyer, L. (1988). Schooling For The Culture Of Democracy. In L. Beyer & M. Apple (Eds.), *The Curriculum: Problems, Politics, And Possibilities*. New York: SUNY. (pp. 219–238).

Bloome, D. (1987). Reading As A Social Process In A Middle School Classroom. In D. Bloome (Ed.), *Literacy And Schooling*. Norwood, NJ: Ablex. (pp. 123–149).

Bloome, D., & Bailey, F. (1992). Studying Language and Literacy Through Events, Particularity, and Intertextuality. In R. Beach, J. Green, M. Kamil, & T. Shanahan (Eds.), *Multidisciplinary perspectives on literacy research*. Urbana, Il.: National Council of Teachers of English.

Christensen, L. (2000). *Reading, Writing and Rising Up*. Milwaukee, WI: Rethinking Schools.

Coles, G. (1998). *Reading Lessons: The Debate Over Literacy*. New York: Hill and Wang.

Cazden, C. (1992). Vygotsky, Hymes, and Bakhtin: From Word To Utterance And Voice. In C. Cazden (Ed.), *Whole Language Plus: Essays On Literacy In The United States And New Zealand*. New York: Teachers College Press. (pp. 190–207).

de Castell, S., & Luke, A. (1986). Models Of Literacy In North American Schools: Social And Historical Conditions And Consequences. In S. de Castell, et al., (Eds.), *Literacy, Society, And Schooling*. Cambridge, UK: Cambridge University Press. (pp. 87–109).

Edelsky, C. (1991). *With Literacy and Justice For All: Rethinking The Social In Language And Education*. New York: Falmer.

Edelsky, C. (1994). *Whole Language: What's New?* (with Bess Altwerger & Barbara Flores). *With Literacy And Justice For All: Rethinking The Social In Language And Education,* Second Edition. Bristol, PA: Taylor and Francis. (pp. 108–126).

Elsasser, N., & Irvine, P. D. (1985). *English and Creole: The Dialectics of Choice in a College Writing Program. Harvard Educational Review*, 55. (pp. 399–415).

Freire, P., & Macedo, D. (1987). *Literacy: Reading The Word And The World*. South Hadley, MA: Bergin & Garvey.

Goodman, K.S., Shannon, P., Freeman, P., & Murphy, S. (1988). *Report Card On Basal Readers*. New York: Richard C. Owen.

Gutierrez, K. (1993). How Talk, Context, And Script Shape Contexts For Learning: A Cross-Case Comparison Of Journal Sharing. *Linguistics and Education*, 5. (pp. 335–365).

Gutierrez, K., Baquedano-Lopez, P., & Turner, M.G. (1997). Putting Language Back Into Language Arts: When The Radical Middle Meets The Third Space. *Language Arts*, 74(5). (pp. 368–376).

Glaser, B., & Strauss, A. (1967). *The Discovery Of Grounded Theory*. Chicago: Aldine.

Graff, H. (1987). *The Legacies Of Literacy*. Bloomington, IN: Indiana University Press.

Heath, S. B. (1983). *Ways With Words*. Cambridge, UK: Cambridge University Press.

Hull, G., Rose, M., Fraser, K., & Castellano, M. (1991). Remediation As Social Construct: Perspectives From An Analysis Of Classroom Discourse. *College Composition and Communication*. 42(3), (pp. 299–329).

Irvine, P. D., & Elsasser, N. (1988). The Ecology Of Literacy: Negotiating Writing Standards In A Caribbean Setting. In G. Rafoth & D. Rubin (Eds.), *The Social Construction Of Written Language*. Norwood, NJ: Ablex.

Knobel, M. (1999). *Everyday Literacies: Students, Discourses, And Social Practice*. New York: Lang.

Larson, J., & Pope, C. (1997, April). Language Arts Textbook Project: A Collaboration With The Rochester City School District. *Research Report*. University of Rochester, Rochester, New York.

Larson, J. & Irvine, P. (1999). We Call Him Dr. King: Reciprocal Distancing In Urban Classrooms. *Language Arts*, 76(5). (pp. 393–400).

Luke, A. (1994). *The Social Construction Of Literacy In The Primary School*. Melbourne, Australia: Macmillan.

Luke, A. (1988). *Literacy, Textbooks, and Ideology: Postwar Literacy Instruction and the Mythology of Dick and Jane*. New York: Falmer Press.

Luke, C., de Castell, S., & Luke, A. (1983). Beyond Criticism: The Authority Of The School Text. *Curriculum Inquiry*, 13(2). (pp. 111–127).

Mehan, H. (1979). *Learning Lessons*. Cambridge, MA: Harvard University Press.

New London Group. (1996). A Pedagogy Of Multiliteracies: Designing Social Futures. *Harvard Educational Review*, 66(1). (pp. 60–92).

Nystrand, M. (1997). Dialogic Instruction: When Recitation Becomes Conversation. In Nystrand, M. (1997), with Gamoran, A., Kachur, R., & Prendergrast, C. *Opening dialogue: Understanding the dynamics of language and learning in the English classroom*. New York: Teachers College Press. (pp. 1–29).

Open Court Reading. (1995). *Collections For Young Scholars*. Peru, IL: SRA/McGraw-Hill.

Perry, T., & Delpit, L. (Eds.) (1997). *The Real Ebonics Debate: Power, Language and the Education of African-American Children*. Milwaukee, WI: Rethinking Schools.

Rist, R. (2000). Student Social Class and Teacher Expectation: The Self-fulfilling Prophecy in Ghetto Education. *Harvard Educational Review*, 70(3). (pp. 266–

301).

Rogoff, B. (1994). Developing Understanding Of The Idea Of Communities Of Learners. *Mind, Culture, and Activity*, 1(4). (pp. 209–229).

Routman, R. (1996). *Literacy At The Crossroads: Crucial Talk About Reading, Writing, And Other Teaching Dilemmas*. Portsmouth, NH: Heinemann.

Scribner, S., & Cole, M. (1981). *The Psychology Of Literacy*. Cambridge, MA: Harvard University Press.

Shannon, P. (1992). Commercial Reading Materials, A Technological Ideology, And The Deskilling Of Teachers. In P. Shannon, (Ed.), *Becoming Political: Readings And Writings In The Politics Of Literacy Education*. Portsmouth, N.H.: Heinemann.

Snow, C., Burns, S., Griffin, P. (1998). *Preventing Reading Difficulties In Young Children*. Washington, D.C.: National Academy Press.

Strauss, A., & Corbin, J. (1990). *Basics Of Qualitative Research: Grounded Theory Procedures And Techniques*. London: Sage.

Street, B. (1995). *Social Literacies: Critical Approaches To Literacy In Development, Ethnography, And Education*. London: Longman.

Strickland, D. (1994). Educating African American Learners At Risk: Finding A Better Way. *Language Arts*. (71)5. (pp. 328–336).

# Chapter Five

## Success Guaranteed Literacy Programs: I Don't Buy It!

*Lynn Asterita Gatto*

Every week my mailbox is stuffed with sales catalogs for foolproof literacy materials and programs. A multitude of companies claim that their workbooks really teach, and their test preparation and practice materials will give students the foundation and practice they need to succeed on standardized tests. Textbook publishers' expensive sales brochures claim their programs will help my students become successful, motivated, confident readers and writers. Even the many professional magazines to which I subscribe are inundated with advertisements for commercial products using "tried and true" methods in order to prepare children for success in literacy. These profit-oriented companies are supported by educators who believe these materials themselves will teach their students to read (Shannon, 1992).

I am a fourth-grade teacher in a mid-sized urban district with twenty-five years of teaching experience. Over those years, I have gained a reputation within my district and around the state as a teacher who is different from most teachers. I have received a number of local and state awards, and most recently I received one of the nation's highest honors for educators: The Presidential Award for Excellence in Science and Mathematics Teaching from the White House. This award identifies outstanding teachers in the country who serve as models and leaders for the improvement of teaching.

As a fourth-grade teacher, I am under great pressure from my district to improve children's test scores. Fourth grade is the first juncture point in New York State at which we administer the high stakes statewide testing that evaluates students in each district for reading, math, and science competencies. When our district's scores are published in the newspapers comparing them to the rest of the county, we are far below the average in all areas. From the superintendent on down to the children, we are all under pressure to perform, which means raising the state and standardized test scores.

Since World War II, literacy has been viewed scientifically, as a subject with a set of skills to be mastered (Coles, 1998; deCastell & Luke, 1983; Shannon, 1992). In response to the pressures of public outcry for higher standardized test scores, my district has taken a strong scientific approach toward literacy and has adopted a total literacy program. This newly purchased program, which each teacher is mandated to use, provides, according to the district and publisher, a complete literacy program that will meet the needs of all our students for successful instruction. In this case, successful instruction equals high test scores. The major component of this new reading program is an anthology of award-winning literature and an accompanying teacher's manual. The manual guides the teacher every step of the way through the skills-based lessons.

In addition to the theme tests for each chapter of the basal, teachers are required to give district written mid-term tests. Teachers must submit the scores to principals, and principals must submit the scores to the school district's central office administrators. The central office administrators believe this total package of instruction and accountability will raise the district's scores and improve the literacy practices of our students. We have become a district dominated by exam-oriented teaching (Street, 1995). But I don't buy it.

According to the state, literacy is defined as reading, writing, listening, and speaking and my district has determined that literacy can be achieved through the accumulation and use of skills and strategies in those areas. My district provides its teachers with a plethora of commercial programs and products in order to teach reading, writing, listening, and speaking. The district expects that all teachers will use the selected reading program they have purchased and that they will do so as described in the teacher's guide. The anthology books are accompanied by skill workbooks, spelling textbooks, phonics workbooks, and handwriting books. Overheads, charts, sentence strips, paperback sets and tapes are also provided as supplemental materials to coincide with the basal program. But I don't use them.

I define literacy as a "shorthand for the social practices of reading and writing" (Street, 1995, p. 2). My approach is to provide experiences and problems that engage students in expanding their existing literacy practices in order to construct and use new ones. Within a community of learner's framework (Rogoff, 1994), I make sure the children in my class have multiple opportunities for literacy events (Heath, 1982) and practices within social contexts. I do not consider myself the giver of knowledge. I view my role as constructing an atmosphere where the children see themselves as valuable to the process of learning within the classroom.

Underlying my teaching is a theory of learning that is grounded in the work of Vygotsky (1978). To this end, I develop units of study that nurture what Nystrand (1997) call "substantive engagement," which he define as a sustained commitment to, and involvement with, academic content and issues (p. 16). It is not enough, however, just for engaging activities to take place; it is equally important for authentic questioning to take place. Nystrand (1997) define such questions as ones that encourage individual interpretations—they open the floor to student ideas for examination, elaboration, and revision (p. 20). Authentic questioning generates in-depth and sustained student conversation, or dialogic instruction as Nystrand (1997) call it.

I encourage dialogic instruction, where the children can express their opinions and disagree with others, self-select the turn-taking during conversation, initiate topics of conversation, offer ideas for activities, and discuss and question concepts (Gutierrez, 1993). These resulting features of dialogic instruction describe a responsive-collaborative script (Gutierrez, Rymes, & Larson, 1995), in contrast to the commercial reading program's script of initiation, response, evaluation, or IRE (Gutierrez, 1993; Mehan, 1979; Nystrand, 1997). Authentic classroom dialogue within a responsive-collaborative script elicits analytical and interpretive responses from the children, unlike IRE where students respond with recitative answers (Nystrand, 1997).

So far, my "Don't" attitude and "I do not use it" conduct have not been challenged by district administration. There are a number of reasons for this. First of all, I have an award from the White House hanging behind my desk! But, even before I received the award, I was considered a successful teacher by the principals for whom I have worked. I must admit, in the last ten years I have transferred out of four schools because of the frequent changes in administration, which left me to work with principals who lacked pedagogical vision and leadership skills. Since my district comprises thirty-nine elementary schools, I have had little difficulty transferring to the schools of my choice.

Each year, my students' state and standardized test score averages surpass the school and district norms (see Irvine & Larson, this volume, for description of district averages). My students' parents are very satisfied with their children's progress and enthusiasm toward school and learning. In my district there is a high rate of mobility, yet my classroom's yearly enrollment is stable. In fact, I have had many parents continue to use their old addresses and drive their children to school every day, even after they have moved out of my school's residence zone, just to keep them in my class. In a school of 730 children, where our average attendance at PTA meetings is five to seven parents, I average twelve to eighteen families out of twenty-one students when I hold a special event. At every schoolwide awards assembly, my class has had significantly more awardees for perfect attendance than any other class. Last semester alone, seven out of twenty-one children received perfect attendance awards.

Although the district administration does not question my methods, I am frequently challenged by my colleagues. When the teachers in my school prepare for a new school year, the textbooks and workbooks are stacked in high piles all over the gym. Everyone vies for the few rolling carts in order to pick up and deliver their heavy load of books. As I walk out with just thirty thin paperback spelling dictionaries, some veteran teacher always asks, "Is that all you're taking? Why aren't you taking your books?"

There have even been times when some helpful colleague delivers the books to me with subtle statements like, "You're going to need these," or "I know you do not like to use books, but the kids will want them." I take them and then return them later to the bookroom. I am asked with incredulous skepticism at least once a month by some teacher, "How can you teach without using the textbooks?" But, there are many other teachers who ask me to share my approach with them. As I present workshops, teach graduate classes, deliver keynote speeches, and write articles, I try to communicate to others what it is I do in the classroom. This is a difficult task; there is so much that I do that seems implicit and intuitive. I have recently entered a doctoral program so that I can better articulate my practice and philosophy to others.

In this chapter, I describe only the literacy practices that focus on reading, writing, listening, and speaking. For reasons of brevity, I have excluded any description of math, science, and social studies, which I also consider part of the literacy practices in my classroom. Furthermore, a discussion of classroom environment and building a community of learners has also been omitted. I would need to write a whole book, not just a chapter!

So, how do I teach without using textbooks within the confines of the district's mandate to use the commercially produced textbook series? This chapter describes how I create a classroom environment rich in literacy practices without using the prescribed textbooks and commercially produced materials. Considering the individual students, planning carefully, selecting appropriate materials and activities, and adjusting activities are all important aspects of what I do to establish a successful literacy program. Luke (1994) describes these decisions as:

> ...a series of inclusions and exclusions, of decisions about what to teach and what not to teach, what can be said and done with written language and what cannot, about what kinds of texts and competencies are appropriate and valuable (p. 20).

None of these decisions need to be made when a basal program is used to teach literacy; they have made all the decisions for teachers. The view I will provide is only a glimpse of my decisions and practice.

This year, I had twenty-two children in my class. The racial makeup of the children in the class was comprised of fourteen African-Americans, six Caucasians, and two students with Spanish surnames. The class was considered heterogeneous, having been organized on the basis of third-grade test scores, although, eight of the children were designated remedial readers, one as special education, and one as ESOL (English for Speakers of Other Languages).

Just as many recent basal programs are organized, my approach also uses themes. However, my themes are for developing motivation for literacy events in my classroom. Unlike the basal programs, where the units are based on such themes as family, fairy tales, super sleuths, meeting the challenge, or immigration, my units are based on authentic activities centered around a theme. Most recently, my fourth-grade students and I completed the planning, constructing, and exhibiting of a walk-in butterfly vivarium (a structure to create conditions for replicating a habitat). This unit was based on introducing and using many new mathematical and scientific concepts, but reading, writing, listening, and speaking permeated every aspect of it.

Many publishers are wise to the integration of subjects and often include what they call "integration connections" sections for each of their themes. But these are just add-ons. I chose the vivarium project because through it the children would need to know about many of the curriculum standards I am required to teach. Describing life cycles and animal habitats, classifying animals, creating environmental awareness, figuring area and perimeter, using averaging, creating models to scale, and drawing blueprints were the science and math concepts that would be used. But, in order to understand any of the math and science, literacy was useful and necessary. In other words, literacy is a practice, something that gets done, not skills to be learned for use at a later date (Oakes & Lipton, 1999; Tharp & Gallimore, 1988).

Before I introduced the project to the children, I checked out every book in the school library on butterflies. The books varied in difficulty from adult field guides and references to picture books. I also searched through magazine issues, both adult and children's, for articles on butterflies. Those reader filmstrips and large picture charts that no one ever uses any more also went into my ever-growing pile of resources. My last stop in the library was to root through the fiction section for any stories that may connect to the theme. By this time in the year, there were many rolling carts available, so I quickly loaded up the cart and headed back to my classroom. I added to these materials by purchasing taped stories on butterflies, videos, models, and coloring and sticker books.

I buy and use very few of the commercial products that promise to teach literacy to my students, but I do buy many materials for my classroom. I spend considerable sums of my personal budget on books, writing supplies, computer and video equipment, subscriptions to children's periodicals, and models. I scour garage sales every summer and shop the dollar stores frequently! I have also gotten quite astute at locating and writing grants (the Toshiba Foundation supported this vivarium project with a $900 grant), to support the purchase of what I consider necessary materials for which my district does not provide. I also borrow extensively not only from the school library, but also from the public library and from other teachers.

I begin every unit by creating an environment for immersion into the topic. Once the butterfly books and periodicals were arranged, pictures posted, and models exhibited, the children began to guess that our next unit would be about butterflies. I confirmed their predictions by announcing my idea of designing, building, and maintaining a butterfly vivarium, to which they enthusiastically and immediately approved. Right away there was lots of chatter among the children. As they posed numerous questions and offered answers and ideas, I struggled to record everyone's words on chart paper.

"Where are we going to build it?" "What are we going to use?" "Is there going to be any furniture inside?" "How are we going to keep the butterflies from getting out?" "How are we going to stop little kids from snatching the butterflies?" "What's the difference between a moth and a butterfly?" "How are we going to get the butterflies?" were just a few of the questions that filled four pages of chart paper. Throughout the unit, we added to the list. The focus for most of the activities in our unit came from the children's questions. Every child knew they had something important to contribute to this unit right from the start.

Next, I passed out copies of Roald Dahl's *James and the Giant Peach* to each child. Many of them had seen the video and emphatically stated that there was no butterfly in the book. They wanted to know what was going on. They had come to rely on having everything we do in the classroom being connected. This was out of character. I wrote the question on chart paper, "Why are we reading a book that has nothing to do with butterflies if we're going to study about butterflies?" and I left it hanging in the front of the room. Although many students were familiar with the novel we were going to read, they now had a purpose. It was no longer just a fairy tale to which they already knew the ending. They were searching for the link to butterflies. The connection between *James and the Giant Peach* and butterflies was that all the supporting characters are insects, which belong to the phylum of insects, as do butterflies. Once the children made the insect connection, I introduced the animal kingdom classification system. The mandated reading program just does not provide this kind of motivation or meaningful connection to content for reading.

And so, our unit had begun with the children's questions, unlike a basal or commercial theme, which begins with the publisher's questions. In fact, the basal series from which I am supposed to teach has a chapter from this same novel as part of the anthology. But, I cannot bear the thought of sharing only one chapter of a great book with children. How could they possibly understand or emulate an author's voice by reading only one chapter of an entire novel?

Actually, this was not the first Roald Dahl book we had read this year. *George's Marvelous Medicine* and *Danny, the Champion of the World* were analyzed by the children as I read them aloud during the first semester. When we finished *James and the Giant Peach*, each child selected from a big box of multiple copies of most of Roald Dahl's books. The school librarian had gathered this huge collection for me by putting out a call to other district librarians. We then formed study groups based on their selections in order to further their understanding of Roald Dahl's authorship. Even though the children met in their small groups, we held whole group discussions to examine their theories about Roald Dahl's writing. The program I am supposed to use does not promote in-depth author studies. How are children supposed to connect with authors and their styles if they do not thoroughly study them?

As the children read daily in their author groups, the children were also gathering many facts about butterflies as they chose the books from the classroom library on butterflies for Silent Sustained Reading (SSR). One way I do use the student anthology from the basal program is to supply the children with their own copy that they keep in their desks. Students may choose any story in the anthology at any time for SSR. I begin and end every day with twenty minutes of SSR, where every child and adult in the room reads silently. I often read books for my classes at the university as my choice for SSR. After a few weeks of watching me use Post-It Notes® for marking important passages in the books I was reading, a few children began to ask for the Post-Its®. I questioned their motives thinking that they just wanted to use them in order to experiment with a new school supply. But instead, they explained they wanted to mark passages and pages for people who might need the information for their individual butterfly reports. Soon, "sticky marking" became standard practice in our classroom.

In the multitude of teacher directions and suggestions of the teacher's guide for the reading program, there is no suggestion for such a practice. Yet, it is something readers do who are reading for information. Not once does this real practice of literacy ever get a mention in the teacher's guide of my basal reading program.

Right after we listed our introductory questions about the butterfly vivarium project we investigated the purchasing of butterfly larvae. One small group of children searched the Internet, another looked through science company catalogs, and a third used the phone book. We placed our order with the company that the children selected by comparing and contrasting the various companies, selections, and prices. Upon the arrival of the butterfly larvae, the children squealed with excitement and conversed eagerly. When all the noise subsided, I asked the children to repeat what I had overheard in the varying conversations. After recording their many comments, predictions, and questions, I focused on "How long it would take until the butterflies would emerge? ," "Where are we going to put them so they wouldn't crawl away? ," "What do they eat?"

Each child received a container with a larvae and an accompanying blank journal book. Just as real scientists, they were going to collect and record as much data about their larva as they could. Each day I used my own larva to model illustrating and labeling, notetaking, and data collecting, such as measuring the length of the larva, and timing how long the wings took to dry out. The children were focused on finding out as much information as they could!

A few days after our larvae arrived, we took a trip to our city zoo. We carefully inspected and took notes on how the bird aviary was designed and set up to create an authentic habitat. It gave the children a vision of what our vivarium might look like and the kinds of things we would need to do in order to simulate a habitat for the butterflies. We also met with the education director, who had an extensive background in working with butterflies. He answered all the children's questions and then posed some of his own for them to think about. He also gave us seeds for some of the essential plants for feeding and stimulating egg laying for the butterflies. He reminded the children to search for the other kinds of plants we would need in our vivarium. We left the zoo with a clear picture of our task ahead.

We spent three weeks working on the planning and designing of the vivarium. First the children drew their own idea of what the vivarium should look like and what materials should be used for construction. After the children viewed one another's drawings, we met as a whole group to establish the important aspects that our vivarium should have. In order to determine the size of our vivarium, small groups calculated the area needed to hold eight people. We conducted a survey to determine the average height of the adults and children in our school so we would know how high the vivarium should be. To determine which materials the vivarium should be constructed from we tested the strength, weight, and flexibility of materials suggested by the children. Pro and con lists were compiled to determine the best possible location within the school for the vivarium. We spent hours coming to consensus on the final plans. Once our plans were final we invited the school custodian and principal to our room to view a presentation of our plan and give their input. With their final approval, we began construction of our 8x8x6 high structure. Every child had a part in the construction of the vivarium.

Throughout the twelve-week unit, the children wrote almost daily. Their journals were filled with records of their larva metamorphosis, research notes for their butterfly reports and information that would be helpful in creating a butterfly habitat, explanations for mathematical thinking, visualizations of the vivarium, notes from our visit to the zoo's aviary, interview notes, reflections of readings, and original stories and poems. Our classroom walls and bulletin boards were covered with students' written books and drawings, essays, letters, group posters, and constructed models.

Throughout all this written work, the question of how to spell a particular word came up frequently. Unlike most teachers across America, I do not give weekly word lists for preparation of Friday's spelling test. Does knowing how to spell all the words on a test once a week exemplify being a good speller? If a child consistently spells well throughout his/her daily writing, then I would consider that child a good speller. So, I ignore the weekly word lists provided by the reading series company and never give weekly spelling tests.

The one item I do order each year is a thin paperback spelling dictionary. This commercial product is one that I do use. It has a page for each letter of the alphabet with a selection of corresponding frequently used words listed down the sides. In the middle of each page are spaced black lines so the children can add words of their choice. The children quickly learn the rule about asking how to spell a word in my classroom: "First the book, then a friend, a good speller next, with the teacher at the end!" In other words, look it up in the speller book, and if it can't be found, then ask two classmates, and only if you cannot get an answer from them, ask the teacher. The bright yellow spelling booklets can be seen in use throughout every day, all year long. But, no one's book is the same, each child's book contains only the words chosen by the child.

I also use a word wall for spelling and vocabulary instruction. Unlike the recent commercial products produced for word walls, I use the words from the children's mistakes or questions. During the vivarium unit I noticed almost every child misusing certain homophones such as "there/their/they're" and "buy/by" quite frequently. I immediately set up a word wall to focus on the kinds of mistakes the children were making. The basal program also provides lessons on homophones, but according to the publisher's timing and selection of words, not based on children's need. Word walls kits are now commercially produced and sold. Such a product is useless to me. How would any company know what words my students need for their writing and reading? I do not even know until it comes up, and it is never the same from year to year.

As our study of butterflies intensified, the monarch's yearly migration patterns became a focus of interest for the class after I shared an article in a popular children's magazine. Next, I introduced a short story titled *Radio Man* (Dorros, 1993), a story of a boy whose parents are migrant workers in the United States. The story clearly made a connection to animal migration patterns and human migration. This story is written in Spanish with the English translation underneath. My two Hispanic students were thrilled to share their reading of the Spanish text with the rest of the class. The sets of paperbacks are the one component of the basal program I do use, but only when they apply to the theme I am teaching.

I then read aloud Jacob Lawrence's, *The Great Migration*. In this famous African-American artist's book, he tells the story of his family leaving the south with many other African-Americans to move north in search of employment. For many days, children reread the story and heard each other's stories about their families' move from the south to the north. It was the perfect opportunity to introduce the difference between immigration and migration when the boy who had recently moved from Jordan to the United States told of his move.

The children's interest in Lawrence's paintings led me to find other books he had illustrated. His books were favorites for SSR for many days, and children placed "dibs" on who would get them next. We also took a trip to our local art gallery to view the two Jacob Lawrence paintings in their collection. Sadly, Lawrence died a few weeks later. When I brought in the full-page obituary from the newspaper, I had to make a trip to the copy machine. Every child wanted a copy of the article.

I am always reading the newspaper for articles to share in order to contextualize the topic of the unit within our community and world events. I have never seen this suggested to teachers in the program's teacher's guide. During this unit I read an announcement in our local newspaper for the opening of the photography exhibit Migration: Humanity in Transition, by the internationally known photographer Sebastiao Salgado. I immediately called to schedule a visit. Due to the graphic nature of the photographs depicting oppression, hunger, and war, the museum officials felt the exhibit may not be appropriate for the children, but I assured them the children would benefit. On the way home from the exhibit, as we sat spread out all over the public bus, the children talked among themselves about what they had seen. That night, for homework, the children wrote their reflections of their visit to the exhibit. Their impressions were personal. One child wrote, "I didn't know that people all over the world migrated. I didn't know that people die when they migrate. I didn't know that people are starving. I'm glad I do not have to migrate."

During the focus on migration, a few students were especially interested in the migration patterns of the monarch butterfly. Actually, I thought they did not believe the monarchs from New York really returned to the same trees in the same Mexican town every single year. They wanted more proof and decided to find it on the Internet (Lankshear & Snyder, 2000). They found a site (MonarchWatch.org) that not only validated the migratory patterns of monarchs, but also described the environmental hazards that caused the destruction and interruption of the monarch's migration. The children wanted to raise money to support the foundation's work in creating a monarch reserve. The rest of the class wanted to help too.

I had them brainstorm some ideas for fundraising. They decided on two projects. They would sell handmade bookmarks (with butterflies, of course!) and hold a raffle. I helped a small group of students search the phonebook for nearby retailers that might donate butterfly knickknacks, and they proceeded to write a letter of request for donations. After addressing the envelopes and mailing the letters, each child took a turn placing a follow-up phone call. The value of all the donations totaled over $250!

I suggested that another way the children might effect a change would be by writing to the Mexican government. The children thought this was a great idea; they had never written to any government before! The children made intelligent suggestions and stated valid reasons for the Mexican government to reduce the heavy traffic and deforestation of the region where monarchs migrate. Their concern and understanding is evident, as in this child's letter:

> Dear Mexican Government,
>     I think that you should just half the tourism in Angangueo, Mexico. I know you are making lots and lots of money from the tourism. If you just let half in the place at one time you will still make lots of money. You can't watch them all at one time and the more tourists, the more dangerous it is for the monarchs. That's why you should cut the tourism in half.

It was about this same time that we were finishing the construction of the vivarium and the reality of the project was becoming apparent. One child commented during a class discussion that "we should make the outside of the vivarium like a museum." When asked for further explanation, he described how a museum has displays and signs, and that's what we should do. Many other ideas followed that initial suggestion, "We could put our models out." "We could put out the microscopes and the kids can look at real butterflies." "We can sell bookmarks and raffle tickets." And so, it was decided we would create a butterfly museum modeled after the museums and zoos we had visited.

In creating the vivarium museum, as we started to call it, the children used the computer for many literacy-based activities. They produced labels, signs, pictures, and short explanations for their ever-growing displays. One child took over, acting as a director, making sure everyone used the same font and size so there would be a professional look to the museum. She kept reminding the others that it has to look like a real museum. From the beginning of the unit I had taken pictures of all our activities, and two girls wanted to use the pictures to make a book showing everything we did. The raffle group used the computer to produce raffle tickets.

Soon our classroom was overrun with all the museum artifacts waiting to be put on display in the hallway surrounding the vivarium. We would be ready to open. But, "How?" asked someone one morning. After much arguing and debating, it was decided that each class in the school would be allowed to sign up for a time to visit. More argument and discussion occurred over "How long should the visits be?" "Which students will be the docents on what days?" "What jobs will the docents do?" and "When do we schedule the visits?" When finally every question was settled to the satisfaction of most, various children used the computers to create forms, schedules, and invitations.

This twelve-week unit involved children and adults working together in order to create the vivarium museum and gain an understanding of many content-related concepts. As the students participated together in this jointly constructed activity, learning was taking place on multiple levels. As the teacher, I learned along with the children. According to Rogoff's (1994) definition, my classroom was a community of learners in which students and teacher work together in goal-directed activity. In "Learning in an Inner City Setting," McNamee (1990) cites one of Gundlach's recommendations for creating a true community of writers and readers is by creating opportunities for a community of speakers and listeners too, something that my students and I accomplish.

During the entire unit, children were given many opportunities to ask questions, argue points, suggest ideas, debate issues, take sides, and challenge one another. But, those opportunities for speaking and listening were usually within the safe confines of our classroom community. The grand opening of the vivarium museum and subsequent exhibition gave the children experience in literacy as a social practice within the context of real life.

Throughout the school year, we made numerous visitations to various museums around the city. During every museum visit we were escorted by docents. The children constructed their own knowledge of what a docent does and knows from their personal interactions with the many docents they met this year. Just like real docents of our city's museums, the children would share their expertise with the public as they escorted visitors through the vivarium museum. They had to communicate with adults, children older than themselves, their peers, and children younger than themselves. They even had to explain and inform the public through the visit and interviews of a local news reporter that came on the morning of our grand opening.

When we watched the afternoon report of our upcoming event for that night, the news station incorrectly reported our school name and the identification of a butterfly. The children's indignation and outrage immediately became cause for action. Two children, selected by the others, called the newsroom and made the director aware of the mistakes and provided the corrections. They were assured that the report would be corrected. However, on the five o'clock and eleven o'clock news that night, the report still ran with the incorrect facts. The children knew then that the news is not always reported correctly. I felt like this was one of the most important lessons the children learned in this unit. They would never read the newspaper or listen to the news with blind faith again. How could any commercially produced textbook reading program teach this to children?

Our grand opening was held in the evening and the children proudly gave tours to their families and central office visitors. They sold bookmarks and raffle tickets, explained how to use the microscopes, and described what could be seen under them, identified the parts and functions of the butterfly using the models, presented the scale models of their vivariums and invited the reading of their letters, essays, journals, and bound butterfly reports. We served butterfly cake, which the children had made earlier in the day by following the directions from a magazine recipe sent in by someone's mother.

Our vivarium museum operated for two weeks, and over 600 children and their teachers visited the museum. Every student had at least four opportunities to present the 45-minute tour. This was their chance to share with an audience their own knowledge about butterflies. It also provided the opportunity for dialogue about butterflies from outside their own classroom community. This experience provided valuable feedback to the children in terms of their own understanding of the content and ability to communicate.

It is a widely held belief that reading and writing must be relevant to children's lives in order for them to develop meaningful literacy practices (Cole, 1985; Luke,1994; McNamee, 1990; Vygotsky, 1978;), which could also be referred to as authentic. Authentic literacy (Oakes & Lipton, 1999) includes activities that allow children to communicate about real things of interest to them. The examples cited in this chapter describe authentic literacy, where the children are producers of knowledge, rather than reproducers of knowledge (Nystrand, 1997). Had I used one of the themes from the mandated reading program, my students would have only reproduced the knowledge the company had outlined for them to learn.

I do give the required district criterion tests, which are the reading programs theme tests, and the district's required mid-year test. I hand in the children's results as directed by the district. But these scores are by no means the way I measure how children's practices of literacy are changing within our classroom community of learners. I keep careful and detailed notes on each child. I record the things children do and say. I often talk to parents about their concerns and observations. I meet with individual children to confer about their writing, and we look for the different practices they are using over time. In fact, I fill out report cards with each child and we decide together what the grades and comments should be. This way report cards are meaningful documents to the children, and when parents receive them, their children can explain and discuss the grades and comments. Parent conferences always include the children, and I always begin each one by having the children talk about their learning. After all, if children are supposed to be responsible for their learning, then we must really make them part of the evaluation process.

I also hand in my plan book twice a year as required by my principal. Although not asked for, I also hand in my thematic unit plans every time I begin a new unit. My vice principal delivered a workbook for the fourth-grade English language arts test at the beginning of the year, telling me they would be very helpful in the children's preparation for the test. I advertised free gifts to all the families that attended Open House. Those workbooks were enthusiastically received by parents. They felt as though they knew what to expect on these well-publicized tests and were being provided specific guidance in helping to prepare their children. I do not prepare children for tests, just for life.

Gee (this volume) also offers an example of a child's experience with literacy practices through an extended and materials rich interaction.

Do commercial literacy programs provide cultural, social, or historical relevance for children? They certainly claim to develop critical readers. But, does any basal reading program include opportunities for critically analyzing bias, historical perspective, factual correctness, and current world and local events in their stories? It seems diversity in publishers' materials really means pictures of children with differing ethnic backgrounds or children with physical challenges, as well as folktales from other cultures. Publishing companies just do not consider classrooms as places where children participate in communities of practice so that children can interact to increase the complexity of their literacy practices (Lave & Wenger, 1991).

Had I chosen to use the prescribed teaching methods from the basal program my district requires, my students would have been denied authentic and meaningful literacy practices. Had I chosen to use the basal reader as my focus for reading, my students would have been denied an understanding and awareness of a meaningful and important aspect of their own or their friends' histories. And, we would have never felt the sadness we experienced as a group when Jacob Lawrence passed away this school year.

Had I used the commercial reading materials my district expects teachers to use, my students would have never written their eloquent letters to the Mexican government pleading for environmental protection of the butterfly habitats. Had I followed the district guidelines for teaching literacy as skill based, my students would have never known literacy as a social practice. By practicing, reading, writing, speaking, and listening within the context of an integrated unit, the fourth-grade drop-off problem described by Gee (this volume) was not a factor for my students. My students ended the school year using more complex literacy practices than when they entered.

Do publishing companies and corporations know what's best for our students? Do teachers feel so powerless that they will allow publishing companies and district officials to tell them how to best provide literacy instruction for their students? Do teachers really believe standardized tests measure teaching and learning? When testing becomes the reason for teaching and learning, it becomes a new parasitic practice (Lave & Wenger, 1991). Is this testing parasite eating away at teachers' personal philosophy of teaching? I refuse to relinquish my beliefs of teaching and learning to commercial enterprise. I believe my students to be literate before they enter my classroom. I use their experiences, interests, history, culture, language, and literacy practices to develop the literacy program in my classroom. The children know they are valued as learners within the community of our classroom. Their ideas and opinions count. Often their questions and suggestions stimulate activities, lessons, or discussions. In my classroom, literacy is the bridge between the exciting and meaningful hands-on unit of study and the minds-on construction of knowledge that is central to providing challenging curriculum.

When teachers take a test-centered approach, their students view literacy not as a process, but as something to test (Nystrand, 1997). Most classrooms using commercial programs for literacy instruction rarely emphasize the process of developing and using literacy practices; instead, they emphasize the skills for increasing literacy as something that can be bought. Shannon (1992) describes teachers and students who use a basal reading series for reading instruction, believing that it has the power to teach (p. 189). He warns that teachers' reliance on commercial reading materials are deskilling teachers.

Commercial programs endorse themselves as foolproof. Who are the fools in foolproof? The companies and districts that align their instruction to commercially produced literacy programs believe it to be teachers! Teachers are not fools. Why do they allow themselves to be considered as such? Why are they becoming deskilled? Teachers do not need commercial publishers and products in order to effectively develop literacy practices in our students.

The implications of teachers developing literacy programs to fit their students instead of fitting their students to the programs are many. First, teachers must assert their beliefs and knowledge in order to do what is right for children. I know many intelligent and hard-working teachers who need to stop asking, "Can we do that?" and just do it!

Principals need to support their teachers by providing funds for what is really needed for meaningful literacy learning. Teachers should not have to spend their own money for materials, and valuable class time should not be spent on fundraisers to pay for field trips. Literacy practices do not just happen inside the school! Principals must also encourage and schedule time for teachers to participate in in-depth professional development and reflection. Principals need to back the teachers in their quest for understanding literacy as social practice and for assisting students in understanding the uses and purposes of literacy.

Reading about theory and literacy practices is not enough for teacher educators to provide for preservice teachers. Modeling the kinds of instructional practices that effectively get children to develop literacy practices needs to occur in teacher training programs too. Preservice teachers must also be exposed to classrooms where literacy is socioculturally situated.

When will teachers, administrators, and teacher educators realize literacy cannot be bought?

# References

Cole, M. (1985). The Zone Of Proximal Development: Where Culture And Cognition Create Each Other. In J.V. Wertsch (Ed.), *Culture, Communication And Cognition: Vygotskian Perspectives*. Cambridge, UK: Cambridge University Press.

Coles, G. (1998). *Reading Lessons*. New York: Hill and Wang.

Dahl, R. (1998). *Danny, the Champion of the World*. New York: Puffin Books.

Dahl, R. (1996). *James and the Giant Peach*. New York. Alfred A. Knopf Books.

Dahl, R. (1981). *George's Marvelous Medicine*. New York. Bantam Books.

de Castell, S., & Luke, A. (1983). Defining Literacy In North American Schools: Social And Historical Conditions And Consequences. *Journal of Curriculum Studies*, 15. (pp. 373–389).

Dorros, A. (1993) *Radio Man*. New York. HarperCollins.

Gutierrez, K. (1993). How Talk, Context, And Script Shape Contexts For Learning: A Cross Case Comparison Of Journal Sharing. *Linguistics in Education*, 5. (pp. 335–365).

Gutierrez, K., Rymes, B., & Larson, J. (1995). Script, Counterscript, And Underlife In The Classroom: James Brown Versus Brown V. Board Of Education. *Harvard Education Review*, 65. No. 3. (pp. 445–471).

Heath, S.B. (1982). *Ways With Words*. Cambridge, UK: Cambridge.

Lankshear, C., & Snyder, I. (2000). *With Green, B. Understanding The Changing World Of Literacy, Technology, And Learning. Teachers And Technoliteracy: Managing Literacy, Technology And Learning In Schools*. St. Leonards, Aus: Allen & Unwin. (pp. 23–47).

Lave, J., & Wenger, E. (1991). *Situated Learning: Legitimate Peripheral Participation*. New York. Cambridge University Press.

Lawrence, J. (1993). *The Great Migration*. New York. HarperCollins Publishers.

Luke, A. (1994). *The Social Construction Of Literacy In The Primary School*. Melbourne, Aus: Macmillan Education Australia.

McNamee, G.D. (1990). Learning in an Inner City Setting. In L. C. Moll, (Ed.), *Vygotsky and education*. Cambridge, UK: Cambridge University Press. (pp. 287–303).

Mehan, H. (1979). *Learning lessons*. Cambridge, MA: Harvard University Press.

Nystrand, M. with Gamoran, A., Kachur, R., & Prendergast, C. (1997). *Opening Dialogue: Understanding The Dynamics Of Language And Learning In The English Classroom*. New York. Teachers College Press.

Oakes, J., & Lipton, M. (1999). *Teaching To Change The World*. Boston. McGraw-Hill College.

Rogoff, B. (April, 1994). Developing Understanding Of The Idea Of Community Of Learners" *Mind, Culture, and Activity*. 1 (4). (pp. 209–229).

Shannon, P. (1992). Commercial Reading Materials, A Technological Ideology, And The Deskilling Of Teachers. In P. Shannon (Ed.), *Becoming Political: Readings And Writings In The Politics Of Literacy Education*. Portsmouth, NH: Heinemann. (pp. 182–207).

Street, B. V. (1995). *Social Literacies: Critical Approaches To Literacy In Development, Ethnography And Education*. London, England: Longman Group Limited.

Tharp, R.G., & Gallimore, R. (1988). *Rousing Minds To Life: Teaching, Learning And Schooling In The Social Context*. Cambridge, UK: Cambridge University Press.

Vygotsky, L.S. (1978). *Mind In Society: The Development Of Higher Psychological Processes*. Cambridge: Harvard University Press.

## ❋ Chapter Six

# Fattening Frogs for Snakes: Virtues for Sale

*Patrick Shannon*

Today in the newspaper was a story of a six-year-old boy who shot dead a classmate while at school. I learned that the boy was from Flint, Michigan, and that he had been living with an uncle for the past few months because at least one of his parents was in jail. The household was reputed to be a drug and gun drop with traffic in both at all hours of the day and night. The shooting was considered deliberate, and the paper implied that the uncle was to blame. It is a tragedy of unspeakable sadness.

In the article below that one was an announcement that Pope John Paul II apologized for the Holocaust which occurred during World War II. Although he stopped short of acknowledging the informal pact between Pope Pius the Twelfth and the Third Reich which sanctioned the final solution of the Jewish problem in return for protection of the Church against Communism, the Pope said that he wanted people to know that the Catholic Church officially recognized that madness and that members of the church had participated.

In the March 2000 *Nation* (Kitman, 2000), I read about how automobile and oil companies conspired to add lead to gasoline throughout most of the twentieth century. Company executives did this although they knew it cost more to make leaded gas and it polluted the environment. In fact, the company had research results early on which suggested that fumes from leaded gas would eventually kill people. Although unleaded gas is now the norm in the United States, multinational oil companies (with significant property and assets in the US) still market leaded gas worldwide. Apparently, it helps car engines run better.

February 25, 2000, a jury acquitted four New York City police officers who killed Amadou Diallo while he reached for his wallet to present identification. The officers admitted to firing forty-one bullets in order to "detain" the West African immigrant. During the trial, the officers said they were young, not well trained for such situations, and scared. They mistook his wallet for a gun and were sorry.

In March 2000, over twenty million Americans watched a Fox

network television show on which a millionaire bachelor picked and married a bride from among fifty contestants whom he had not met. *Who Wants to Marry a Millionaire*? Enough said.

Morals matter. We have to make decisions (individually and collectively) on what is right and what is wrong, and we have to act on them. We must choose, no matter how much we may reserve judgment on our actions afterwards. How we come to represent those decisions to ourselves in terms of principles and codes of action that will act as guidelines for future action become plays of power with myriad consequences. Which and whose morals matter? Should the alleged drug and gun dealing of the uncle or General Motor's systematic destruction of the economy of Flint present the greater moral dilemma for us? Should we feel relieved that the Pope acknowledged the Catholic Church's complicity or question the timing of his remarks? Is all fair in love and business? Whose morals influenced the NYPD's actions and the jury's deliberation? Who wants to marry a millionaire? Is it the questionable acts of individuals and institutions which drive our interest in morals or is it our own willingness to sit back and watch these questionable acts without reaction, which leads us to rethink our moral standing?

Our values take front stage in our answers to these questions. What do we want? How do we want to live together? Our answers to such questions locate us within complex networks of group memberships (or discourses) (Hall, 1992). Our answers—that is, our values—identify us as members of particular groups that are subject to strictures imposed from within and without the group (Gee, 1992). The Pope recognizes little irony in his seventy-years-too-late apology. General Motors, executives suggest that it's just business that ruined the Flint economy. The boy's uncle believes that children should raise themselves. The millionaire practices acquisition; the bride has faith in Hollywood romance. Each is content with his or her answers, his or her values. Outside these groups, we may have different answers and points of view which challenge the morals of these protagonists, but within the groups there are few who raise such questions. Which groups' values dominate in particular situations are more matters of power than Truth (Foucault, 1972). To see these complexities in the discussions of current events is not to advocate a relativist position on morals. Rather it is to recognize that the world is a complex set of peoples and places in which multiple sets of morals coexist, compete, and sometimes conflict (Cherryholmes, 1999). Many groups have written sets of "rules" to guide moral behavior. For example, the Bible lists ten codes, including:

Thou shall not kill, but the Catholic Church sanctioned killing and so did that jury.

Thou shall not steal, but oil companies stole the health of millions of Americans and continue to take the health of many around the world.

Thou shall not covet thy neighbor's wife, but Fox was in a sweeps month.

When we ask questions about why people chose the actions they did in specific situations, we define the fact that morals matter in pedagogical terms. Our questions demonstrate our wonder about the content of the decisions made or the actions taken, and our concern over the manner in which participants learned to make such choices and to take such actions. Our questions imply that we hope for change from current moral practice to ones which more closely resemble what we value. For example, when we question General Motors' decisions to remove its factories from Flint without regard for the action's effects on those living in Flint, we imply that business should always keep people in mind as it works toward profit. By definition, the intent to affect other's thoughts, beliefs, values, and actions is pedagogical. The effort to find/practice effective moral pedagogy is as old as educational writing— my membership in the old white guy academics group suggests that this writing began with the Ancient Greeks, but members of other groups, academic or not, may suggest other points of origin. For example, many members of the liberation movements culminating in the second half of the twentieth century offer alternative moral and pedagogical points of reference, placing women as well as men, people of color as well as white, and poor as well as rich at the center (Black Panther Party Platform, 1966; Fraser, 1997; Hooks, 1989; Redstocking Manifesto, 1969; SNCC Speaks for Itself, 1966; Welch, 1985; West, 1993). Each group (including mine) seeks to further its values, and many vie for a predominant role in moral education in and out of schools.

Into this moral and pedagogical quandary leap the moral entrepreneurs, naming absolute virtues and selling curricula to develop more moral Americans (Nash, 1997). These entrepreneurs transform morals into things for sale (commodities), moral concern into markets, and moral pedagogy into commercialized practice. Rather than oddities, these transformations are natural developments of capitalism, in which new markets for new products must be continuously developed without regard for time, place, or the people involved. At least since the 1980s, protections against the incursion of capitalism into more and more of our everyday lives have been curtailed because neoliberalism has captured the imaginations of many public (and private) officials (Greider, 1998).

As the contributors to this volume suggest, however, not all are convinced that unchecked capitalism offers a livable future for most people. There are signs of dissent outside this book as well. We see these signs in the angst of workers who fear loss of employment to merger, downsizing, or subcontracting (Sklar, 1995), in the loud lament of the loss of civic participation (Putnam, 2000), in the odd coalition between Ralph Nader's and Phyllis Schlafly's political groups to fight the commercial exploitation of children, in the campus movements to end sweatshops worldwide, and in the demonstrations in Seattle and Melbourne against the World Trade Organization and in Washington D.C. against the World Bank and I.M.F.

In this chapter I intend to explore the transformations of virtue and pedagogy into commodities through an examination of one entrepreneur's efforts. Although there are now many working the virtue markets in homes and schools (e.g., Bill Honig, William Kilpatrick, Thomas Lackoma, Keven Ryan), none is more visible and successful than William J. Bennett, former Secretary of Education and Drug Czar for the Reagan and Bush administrations and now research fellow at the Heritage Foundation and businessman. I chose Bennett's work because (1) he includes explicit representations of the transformation of virtues into things for sale, moral concern into markets, and pedagogy into a commercial action; (2) he wears his values on his sleeve; and (3) he offers little qualification in his agenda to normalize his values as American values. By looking at those representations—those commodities—we can see the problems Bennett represents and furthers as well as some possible ways we might check his and other moral entrepreneurs' social and economic strategies. Toward that end, I begin with a brief discussion of the concept of commodity because:

> The wealth of those societies in which the capitalist mode of production prevails, presents itself as 'an immense accumulation of commodities,' its unit being a single commodity. Our investigation must therefore begin with the analysis of a commodity." (Marx, 1967, p. 35)

## Commodities and Fetishism

A commodity appears to be for many people just an object, a thing. That thing has a double nature, however. That is, it has use-value (bringing utility and/or pleasure to people) and exchange-value (commanding other objects or money in transactions of daily life). While use-values are a product of both labor and nature (social and physical entities), exchange values are purely social constructs established as ratios of comparable labor among the objects to be exchanged. (This labor theory of value was accepted by Aristotle and Adam Smith despite Milton Friedman's pretense that it was a communist plot.) To make labor comparable across commodities, it must be reduced to a common kind, as undifferentiated and measurable as any other thing involved in commercial production. The human activity of work then must be separated from personal expression or development in order to become one of many comparable factors to be considered in the manufacture of things for sale. This need for "abstract" labor requires a particular set of circumstances in which profit is the highest priority in the production of commodities.

That set of circumstances, capitalism, organizes production in such a way to reduce the costs of production to a minimum (in order to maximize profits). This profit motive impels capitalist manufacturers to seek a "division of labor" (as Adam Smith named it)—a historically specific method of reducing individualized and differentiated work into routine and regular acts, creating new efficiencies. The profit drive, then, creates the powerful forces to homogenize labor and to simplify its form in order to imbue the commodity with the capacity for exchange. Under capitalism, even labor becomes a commodity—a thing that individuals possess, develop, and sell in order to survive and perhaps thrive. Despite its simple appearance as an object, commodities represent all these invisible social relationships.

Marx called the invisibility of these relationships "the fetishism of commodities." By this he meant that we lose sight of the social character of commodities and act as if the physical properties of the commodity command a price. Many (even some) economists believe that the thing itself has the power to establish an object's price, and not the human labor or the social construction of exchange value. Thus, as Marx writes, a "definite social relation between men themselves...assumes...the fantastic form of a relation between things" (1967, p. 165). Capitalism's (im)moral character is based on this fetishism of commodities—this distortion of reality.

For example, when land and capital used in production are fetishized, they seem to command remuneration through profits because of their physical properties. (Marx described it, "an enchanted topsy-turvy world, in which Monsieur le Capital and Madame la Terre do their ghost walking as social characters and at the same time as mere things," 1967, p. 169.) Upon inspection, however, it is the rights accorded to the owners of land and capital (by governments through laws) which enables owners to exert a claim on production (on behalf of the contribution to output made by "their" resources or capital goods that is the productive element).

The confusion between this social right and the physical reality of productivity—a central part of the fetishism—obscures the workings of capitalism from public view. It appears that the things—land, machines, etc.—are being remunerated with profits for their contributions, and not their owners, who are accumulating profits. In a sense, however, the transfer is an act of stealing. The physical parts of production are transformed from one state to another, but the surplus value which labor creates (beyond laborers' remuneration) is taken from the laborers. Under capitalism, this government-sanctioned robbery is deemed acceptable (even necessary) by the most precise "scientific" inquiry (economics) (Heilbronner, 1985). Through their research, economists endeavor to understand the nature of the system and to naturalize its social and personal values. With government and science behind it, capitalism projects the illusion that it is the natural state of civilization which we must preserve at all costs—James Madison's interpretation of that famous phrase—"the pursuit of happiness." Once land, capital, and labor are transformed into commodities and those commodities are fetishized, all subversive interpretations of the system disappear.

Each commodity that we encounter, then, can teach us about capitalism as a socially constructed, historical system of production. There is nothing eternal or natural about capitalism (although there are universals within it and a recognizable order to its system). When we consider the commodification of public and private life we must remember its social construction, and not just dwell only on the immediate appearance and illusion of the new commodity created. The values directing that construction include the central role of profits in the structures and practices of our daily life, the rights of owners of the means of production to all the profits from commodity exchange, the notion that laborers must be alienated from their work in order to achieve the highest exchange-values for commodities, and the fact that anything, one practice or idea can become a commodity. Everyone must accept these values in order for capitalism to continue (Marcuse, 1993). The stronger the acceptance of the values and the roles they imply for each citizen, the easier it is for capitalism and capitalists to prosper.

At a cultural level, commodities represent the values of their manufacturers (Schor, 2000). The thing for sale is an embodiment of not only generalized values of capitalism but also of what manufacturers want in the world and how they wish to live with others. Manufacturers produce commodities for profit, of course, but also enter production to make the world better (according to their vision of better). This may seem hard to accept with so many cynical commodities on the market (chocolate cereals, handguns, cigarettes, Elvis statues, etc.). Cereal manufacturers point to the importance of choice in the development of individuals and to the aid that they bring to parents who struggle to get their children to eat breakfast (vitamin contents are displayed on the side of the box). Handgun producers trot out the second (the right to bear arms) and fourth (freedom from unlawful search and seizures) Amendments to the US Constitution. Beyond the basic acceptance of capitalism, each commodity expresses its manufacturer's commitment to a freedom of choice, to a quality of life, and to an ideal of how the world should work (Lear, 1994). Even manufacturers who consciously make and sell products they know to be harmful display their values about how the world should work and their elevated position in that world. For example, as John Edgar Widemann (1995) suggests about those who propose barbaric prison conditions, these manufacturers do not believe that their products are produced for people like themselves.

The appeal to values can be used by manufacturers to develop brand loyalty. That's why we see so many American flags in advertisements. To an extent, perhaps, this appeal to values is only a sales strategy, but it is also a declaration of the manufacturer's defining features. These values express how they wish to be known and what they believe about themselves (Bourdieu, 1984). Often their espoused values lie in direct conflict with principles of capitalism—lowest costs and highest profits. For example, the Wal-Mart officials contradicted their own "Made in America" campaign because the cost of imported products was less for the company. Nike and other sports apparel manufacturers have been caught in similar contradictions. Consumer advocates exploit this tension by proposing product loyalty if manufacturers will abide by a more people-friendly moral code in their conception, production, and marketing of commodities. Much of the effort around the campus protests against university contracts with companies that use sweatshop labor follow this lead to reveal the realities of capitalism at the turn of the twenty-first century.

To understand the commercialization of moral values, then, we must examine the commodities offered, the markets created, and values promoted through the extension of capitalism into private matters. As with any commercial venture, it's important to understand how production is financed, to whom products are marketed, and what is being sold. I turn to Bennett's efforts in this enterprise.

## Marketing Virtue

With the help of the federal government, the Public Broadcasting System, scores of research assistants, the Heritage Foundation, and many other conservative groups (e.g., Focus on Family, Eagle Forum, Olin Foundation, and the Hudson Institute), William J. Bennett has produced over thirty commodities of virtue. His efforts began with government service as Director of the National Endowment for the Arts and Humanities during the Reagan Administration. Aiming at higher education, his report *To Reclaim a Legacy* sets several of the tenets of his project. "Although more than 50 percent of America's high school graduates continue their education at American colleges and universities, few of them can be said to receive there an adequate education in the culture and civilization of which they are members" (1984, p. 1). In this title and short proclamation, Bennett names several of his values, begins to create a market, and implies a solution to a social problem (albeit, not a commercial one). That is, he names a singular definition of culture and civilization (the legacy), he concludes that colleges and universities are inadequate and damaging our youth, and he suggests that attention to this crisis is required. Eight years later in his memoir of his work for the Reagan and Bush administrations, he made this charge more bluntly. "We are in the midst of a struggle over whose values will prevail in America" (1992, p. 9).

At first consideration, it may seem ungenerous to suggest that Bennett's efforts in this struggle are the commodification of virtue, but his relentless generation of new products (books for adults, anthologies for adults and kids, recorded versions of both; a television show; a Website, books from the Website, dolls from the television and Website, etc.) makes me curious about his intention. Moreover, Bennett's reply that he didn't take a vow of poverty when he was asked if he would continue in the second Bush administration (if there had been one), pushes me toward that conclusion. His salary as a government official (which is public record) was well over $100,000 per year, with a generous expense account. During those years of "poverty," Bennett honed his argument and vigorously attempted to create a market for virtue education by promoting the notion that all levels of the American education system, from preschool to graduate, were inadequate and dangerous—not just for the young, but for all Americans.

*Our Children and Our Country* (1988) presents twenty-four speeches that Bennett made to various groups while he served as Secretary of Education. It is interesting to compare his subjects and tone across these speeches. Although Bennett enjoys his reputation as a "straight-talker". he has an acute sense of audience. For the National Press Club, he announced his intention to bring the three Cs—content, character, and choice—to the forefront of discussions about education. He concluded that elementary schools were "doing pretty well," and secondary schools and colleges were missing opportunities to capitalize on this strong start.

Yet, when he addressed the Focus on Family group, he stated, "If the family fails to teach honesty, courage, desire for excellence, and a host of other skills, it is exceedingly difficult for any other agency to make up for its failures" (p. 63). To the Eagle Forum, he worries that high school students distrust the federal government and are not certain of its superiority to that of the Soviet Union and concludes that "Those who claim we are now too diverse a nation, that we consist of too many competing convictions and interests to instill common values, are wrong" (p. 75).

His speech at the Manhattan Institution in 1986 names his solution to these problems—moral literacy. Comparing moral literacy to E.D. Hirsch's cultural literacy (the argument that Americans must have a common knowledge of facts in order to communicate with each other), Bennett concludes "if we want our children to possess the traits of character we most admire, we need to teach them what those traits are. They must learn to identify the terms and content of those traits." True to his conservative convictions, Bennett maintained that teaching moral literacy does not require new courses or more funding. Rather existing English and history classes could be redesigned to fit this need. "We have a wealth of material to draw on—material that virtually all schools once taught to students for the sake of shaping character" (p. 81). This redesign will be driven by "a grassroots movement for education reform that has generated a renewed commitment to excellence, character, and fundamentals" (p. 9). By the end of the 1980s, Bennett had extended the market for moral education beyond his conservative constituency by tying it to individual development and general social and economic security.

During the 1990s, Bennett released a series of books intended to spread his interpretation of the causes of this social decline. The titles convey their content: *The De-Valuing of America* (1992*), The Index of Leading Cultural Indicators* (1994), *Body Count* (1996), *The Death of Outrage* (1998), and the millennium issue of *The Index of Leading Cultural Indicators* (1999). Although each book offers some unique information, all present Bennett's theme developed during the 1980s when speaking to conservative groups—liberal American institutions are not prepared or willing to deal with the social problems released during the morally bankrupt 1960s and 1970s. At that time, Bennett charges, American standards on drugs, promiscuity, divorce, crime, popular culture, and laziness were ruptured by minority groups attempting to gain social recognition and redistribute cultural and economic wealth in the United States. The result, Bennett concludes, is a society in which more and more people lack impulse control and empathy for others. This de-valuing led to an America in which citizens can no longer feel secure in public or even in their homes.

Bennett disparages both conservative and liberal solutions to these growing social problems. He suggests that advocates for prisons without compassion, the death penalty, and more guns are concerned only with curtailing the consequences of social ills, and not with addressing their causes. Extreme conservative solutions—debtor prisons for the lazy, death to the sexually active (through HIV), or more guns for citizens do not adequately deal with issues that concern Bennett. Conservative advocates of these solutions are not interested in irradiating the problems, he charges. Although he laments the conditions in which some people live and the isolated incidents of bias a few Americans suffer, Bennett maintains that poverty and racism are no longer serious problems in America. Moreover, he suggests that the economic opportunities in America at the turn of the century make poverty inexcusable. Those opportunities and the laws prohibiting discrimination make racism a poor choice for those interested in America. That is, liberal explanations for social problems and the solutions they propose are outdated and just do not make sense.

Bennett offers individual character as the cause of all social ills, and he coins the term "moral poverty" to make his point.

> Moral poverty is the poverty of being without loving capable responsible adults who teach right from wrong; the poverty of being without parents or other authorities who habituate you to feel joy at others joy, pain at others pain, satisfaction when you do right, remorse when you do wrong; the poverty of growing up in a virtual absence of people who teach morality by their own everyday example and who insist that you follow suit (1996, p. 27).

This statement of the cause of social problems implies the solution— adults must teach the young to be moral, and newly moral citizens will refrain from antisocial behaviors. Every American citizen, then, is engaged in one way or another with explicit moral education.

For much of the 1980s and 1990s, Bennett wrote for a moral majority whom he assumed shared his concerns for society. Many of his speeches and early essays relied on rhetorical forms of inclusion— "When the American people are asked what they want from schools, they consistently put...help them to develop reliable standards of rights and wrongs that will guide them through life" (1988, p. 9). *Body Count* appears to be written for a suburban and rural audience who feared the unknown of cities, which Bennett populates with "juvenile super- predators, radically impulsive, brutally remorseless youngsters" (1996, p. 27). In most of his books, Bennett is sure of his audience, preaching first to the choir, and then, to the easily converted. Yet with the public charges of scandal during the Clinton Administration, Bennett seemed startled to find that many Americans did not seem to be alarmed. Amid the longest economic expansion in American history, a majority were willing to overlook "political" indiscretions. In *The Death of Outrage: Bill Clinton and the Assault on American Ideals* (1998), Bennett chides that majority to be "angry at the proper things and the proper people." The lack of outrage, Bennett claims, is a sign that things are worse than he thought—most Americans are morally illiterate or at least alliterate.

## Virtues as Commodities

If the moral decline of the United States is a fact according to the index of leading cultural indicators, then virtue is not apparent to all Americans. If the moral character of the nation is to be raised, then virtue must be named, described, and demonstrated. Although Bennett had listed virtues in his speeches and books of the 1980s, his efforts to raise the moral character of America began in earnest with *The Book of Virtues: A Treasury of Great Moral Stories* (1993). There he announced that self-discipline, compassion, responsibility, friendship, work, courage, perseverance, honesty, loyalty, and faith are the essential American virtues. To avoid confusion over what these labels might mean, he offered a singular definition for each based on his reading "the corpus of Western Civilization, that American schoolchildren once upon a time, knew by heart" (p. 15). Although Bennett warned that virtues are not like "beads on a string or marbles in a pouch" that can be possessed, he maintained that these ten will supply the moral anchoring for each American. In order to obtain these anchors, Bennett invites all to read the stories he placed in his anthologies: "Parents will discover that reading this book with or to children can deepen their own, and their children's, understanding of life and morality" (p. 14).

The structure of *The Book of Virtues* is simple because Bennett believes that the morals reside in the text itself. After a very brief introduction (taken almost verbatim from the Manhattan Institution speech), each virtue receives a chapter—a two-page introduction/ definition followed by scores of short stories, poems, letters, excerpts, and fables on that theme. Through the shear weight of repetitive example, Bennett assumes that readers will be convinced of the value of these virtues. Moreover, once valued, readers can habituate themselves toward each virtue by "marking favorite passages, for reading aloud to family, for memorizing pieces here and there" (p. 15). Readers then have "specific reference points…and a stock of examples illustrating what we see as right and wrong, good and bad—examples illustrating that, in many instances, what is morally right and wrong can indeed be known and promoted" (p. 12). Bennett uses a metaphor—the chapters as rich quarries of virtues, which readers are to mine—in order to portray the effort and reward in this character education. Upon completing all the chapters, readers become morally literate, good Americans.

Bennett's message proved wildly popular, as *The Book of Virtues* spent over a year on the *New York Times* best-seller list. As a commodity, *The Book of Virtues* promised to bring virtues to those who purchased it. If the approved virtues were indeed in the texts waiting to be discovered, then the virtues are for sale—things to be acquired through a two-step process. First, buy the book, and then, read the book morally. Owning and reading *The Book of Virtues* makes the virtues property to be used at the morally literate owner's discretion. Lost in the fetishism of this commodity is the human center of moral education. The possible value of interaction between text author (Bennett only wrote 26 of the 831 pages in the book) and reader is subsumed in the abstraction of the singular correct interpretation of each text read. The text—the thing—seems to be the moral agent, not the author or reader. And Bennett is ready to sell that thing (in multiple forms) to every family and every schoolteacher.

For $30 (hard cover), Bennett offers virtues which favor his interpretation of America as the last best hope of Western Civilization. The dust jacket presents affirmations for the book from Margaret Thatcher, Rush Limbaugh, and Roger Staubach, suggesting the political slant of the virtues inside. Bennett's selection of virtues is skewed in favor of his conservative political agenda. Although he quotes Plato frequently and he declares that his virtues reflect the best of Western Civilization, Bennett does not even follow Plato's lead. Plato distinguished four cardinal virtues: wisdom, courage, temperance, and justice. Bennett ignores Plato's intellectual virtue, wisdom, and reinterprets his political one, justice. For example, Bennett suggests that Frederick Douglas's 1852 Fourth of July speech on the hypocrisy of celebrating Independence Day in a slave nation is about responsibility; he selects courage as the virtue of Susan B. Anthony's symbolic vote in the 1872 presidential election; and he characterizes Mary Wollstonecraft's (1792) *A Vindication of the Rights of Women* as a demonstration of faith.

Bennett admits that "Some of the history that is recounted here may not meet the standards of the exacting historian. But we tell these familiar stories as they were told before, in order to preserve their authenticity" (p. 14). Bennett's assignment of virtues to the texts he includes, however, is more than a historical quibble. His representations of history repackage our present as well as our past. When we encounter another text about apartheid (Douglas's point), democracy (Anthony's point), or women's rights (Wollstonecraft's point), Bennett wants us to direct our attention away from issues of justice in order to find his main ideas of responsibility, courage, and faith. According to Bennett, Americans should strive to be self-disciplined, responsible, honest, loyal, faithful, and to work and persevere, but not to be wise or seek justice.

Bennett's selected texts convey much more than he is willing to admit. Consider his use of Abraham Lincoln's letter to Mrs. Bixby of Boston in the compassion section (p. 177). Lincoln believed that Mrs. Bixby's five sons were killed while fighting for the Union armies. In the introduction to the letter, Bennett quotes Carl Sandburg, a Lincoln biographer, "the letter wore its awful implication that human freedom so often was paid for with agony" in order to direct readers' interpretation. Lincoln wrote:

> ...I feel how weak and fruitless must be any word of mine which should attempt to beguile you from the grief of a loss so overwhelming. But I cannot refrain from tendering you the consolation that may be found in the thanks of the republic they died to save. I...leave you...the solemn pride that must be yours to have laid so costly a sacrifice upon the alter of freedom.

Bennett suggests that the letter shows Lincoln's compassion. And it may. But the letter is also self-serving. Mrs. Bixby lost sons to a war which Lincoln declared in order to prevent southern states from seceding during his administration—a war which required the service of only those who could not buy their way out of the draft and in which over 600,000 working-class men and boys were killed. In Bennett's efforts to demonstrate the pettiness of those who have challenged the accuracy of many of the documents he included in his book, he reports that Lincoln had been misinformed about the Bixby boys. Two were killed, one was taken prisoner, and two deserted. Clinging to his agenda, Bennett wrote, "Mrs. Bixby's loss and sacrifice hardly could have been greater."

Although I think that Lincoln's letter would be better assigned to the responsibility section, I do not believe that teaching virtue was Bennett's primary objective when he chose Lincoln's letter to repackage history for us. Rather than responsibility, courage, loyalty, or any other virtue he might name, his real purpose seems to be to prepare children and their parents for the next war that Congress declares or for the many conflicts to which our presidents send our sons and daughters. Bennett frames the Lincoln letter to tell readers to forget those deserters and think about the glory of the "sacrifice upon the alter of freedom." A similar agenda runs through several of his books subsequent to *The Book of Virtues. Our*

*Country's Founders (1998), Our Sacred Honor (1997), The Spirit of America (1998), The Children's Book of America (1998), and The Children's Book of Heroes (1997)* shy away from issues of justice so prevalent in our history and embrace a sense of duty to country.

Bennett's sense of duty includes the values of capitalism as well as those of conservative patriotism. He presents the case for capitalism through five virtues: self-discipline, responsibility, work, perseverance, and loyalty. The first order of this business is to reign in our passions and impulses in order to be in control of ourselves. Self-discipline in Bennett's hands becomes a self-surveillance based on accepted social virtues. If we fail with our self-discipline by acting inappropriately, Bennett implores us to take responsibility for our actions. We alone are responsible for who we are, what we do, and why we do it. We must not be idle. "Even sleeping can be a form of investment if it is done for the sake of future activity. But sleep, like amusement, can also be a form of escape—oblivion sought for its own sake rather than for the sake of renewal" (p. 347). Bennett's answer for idleness is to work, and remember "there are no menial jobs, only menial attitudes. And the control of our attitudes are up to us" (p. 348). Self-disciplined and responsible in our work, we must persevere— "the world is lost through hesitation, faltering, wavering, vacillating, or just not sticking with it" (p. 528). Finally, we must be loyal even though "we do not have to like those to whom we are loyal, and they do not have to like us" (p. 666).

Separately, these virtues appear to direct readers along noble paths of reason that might indeed serve the individual (and society) in continuous reflection and development. Collectively, however, these five virtues seem pointed toward compliant workers who will monitor mind and body in continuous service to some larger entity. Moreover, these workers recognize that they are individually responsible for their fate and that they must retain a positive attitude even if they do not enjoy their situation. With these values, workers show up for work daily, ready, willing, and able to do what they are asked; they do not hesitate or question the authority or conditions of their work; they do not ask for more money, more time, more safety; and they remain in their work regardless of how they are treated. Unions are out of the question because they violate loyalty and responsibility. Bennett's moral literacy is a capitalist enterprise in more ways than one.

According to Bennett's logic, by buying *The Book of Virtues*, Americans possess the virtues that will stymie the moral decline since the 1960s, strengthen the national resolve to defend the country's ideals, and enhance the nation's economic performance. Those who need to accumulate more virtue can purchase Bennett's *The Moral Compass* (1996) or any of Bennett's children's books, which set excerpts from these anthologies within Michael Hague's painted illustrations (Bennett, 1995, 1996, 1997). To display these possessions in order to be recognized as a good morally literate American, readers must habituate the examples from the texts in order to change first their own and then others' behavior.

## Character Development as Commercialized Practice

Although Bennett follows Plato's ideas about essential human nature and the realm of well-defined, abstract, and universal moral truths, he begins and ends his moral pedagogy with Aristotle's notion of moral behavior as habit. Human beings become virtuous by imitating adult examples in everyday life. This strange mix places remarkable demands on adults. On the one hand, adults must be clear in imparting the essence of each virtue (found in Bennett's books), but on the other hand, they must apply those virtues in the complexities of their lives. The first demand requires adults to use deduction to identify the morals in Bennett's text (this is relatively simple because Bennett labels each text). The second demand is much more difficult. Aristotle's empiricism requires self-critical, relativistic, reversible logic to induce what's right in any particular situation. According to Aristotle, that reasoning is the habit of character to be formed. Within Bennett's pedagogy, adults face the challenging task of reconciling the absolute nature of morals and the particulars of their application. Rather than accept this challenge, however, Bennett rejects its importance.

The reader scanning this book may notice that it does not discuss issues like nuclear war, abortion, creationism, or euthanasia. This may come as a disappointment to some. But the fact is that the formation of character in young people is educationally a different task from, and a prior task to, the discussion of the great, difficult ethical controversies of the day. First things first. And planting ideas of virtue, of good traits in the young, comes first. In the moral life, as in life itself, we take one step at a time. Each field has its complexities and controversies. And so too does ethics. And each field has its basics. So too with values. This is a book in the basics. The tough issues can, if teachers and parents wish, be taken up later. And I would add, a person who is morally literate will be immeasurably better equipped than a morally illiterate person to reach a reasoned and ethically defensible position on these tough issues (p. 13).

After the complexities of life are removed from consideration, what remains in Bennett's moral pedagogy is the notion that absolute morals can be learned by rote and that the application of those absolutes is relatively straightforward. And this is where Bennett's commercialized pedagogy becomes apparent. He has established that American culture is in decline, that adults (teachers and parents) are not always cognizant of the absolute morals needed to stop this decline and return America to moral greatness, and that currently no institution has accepted responsibility to teach character. In order to fill this void, Bennett offers two sets of commodities to direct moral pedagogy. First, he publishes a series of anthologies and picture books to impart the absolute morals, and second, he produces the PBS series, Website, and storybooks from the PBS episodes in order to provide adults with simplified daily life examples.

The animated PBS show, *Adventures from the Book of Virtues*, began its third year of production in 2000. These adventures take place in a fictional world of Spring Valley, where preadolescents Zach and Annie ride bicycles to Plato's Peak and encounter talking animals. Plato (a buffalo, which is presumably Bennett), Aristotle (a prairie dog), Socrates (a mountain lion), and Aurora (an eagle) present tales (similar to the story texts in *The Book of Virtues*) which address the moral dilemmas which Zach and Annie face. In each case, the issues are clear-cut and simple and the morals of the stories fit perfectly. When the children return home, they know exactly how to solve their problems. None of the problems are intended to signify morally anomalous situations; for example, when the virtue of honesty conflicts with the virtue of compassion or when courage is incompatible with expressions of loyalty or faith. The episodes imply that life is simple to understand once you know which moral examples to apply in each situation. Bennett has been part of the production since its inception. Although he does not draw the cartoons or write the stories, he has copyrighted all of the characters, which he leases to the production company.

By buying these commodities (PBS will sell you *The Children's Book of Virtues* and six videotaped episodes of the *Adventures from the Book of Virtues* for $74.88), teachers and adults can provide the moral curriculum for children, themselves, and the country. Reading and memorizing the ten virtues, learning to ignore complexity in moral dilemmas, and applying the appropriate virtue to the simplified problem makes one morally literate. Lost in this commercial exchange are the moral reasoning of the authors of these texts and the possible discussions of meaning that readers might construct from the texts (and the contexts). The texts, not the authors, bring the morals, and Bennett, not the adult present at the reading, brings the meaning of the texts. Bennett's re-presentation of virtue as text consumption and teaching as transportation of correct meaning to impressionable but docile minds makes moral pedagogy an exchange between things (not people). Bennett's work positions readers (us) in the overlap between conservatism and capitalism—a rough spot for anyone except the wealthy.

Bennett's claim that his moral curriculum becomes more sophisticated as children age rings hollow. It appears that the moral literacy of the PBS show and *The Book of Virtues* are the beginning and the end of his pedagogy. In *The Educated Child: A Parent's Guide From Preschool Through Eighth Grade* (1999, written with Chester Finn and John Cribb), Bennett offers character education under the chapter heading "Along with Academics." Although the recommended texts for different disciplines increase in complexity, Bennett presents no clear plan for increasing the complexity of students' moral literacy. His checklist to determine if a child's school is performing well is to quiz students on specific facts. (Quick: What happened in 1789? There's only one correct answer, and it's not the storming of the Bastille.) The only explicit moral guidance offered to teachers and parents is that students should be told not to take drugs, not to have sex, not to watch television, or listen to rock and roll.

## Fixed Virtues vs. Democratic Demands

As the stories in the introduction demonstrate, everyday life is not as simple as Bennett would have it. For all his attempts to deny the complexities of children's lives, he writes from a position of naiveté and privilege. Bennett's children (who appear in the book jacket photos) are not touched by violence, religious duplicity, corporate greed, racism, and sexism in their daily lives. Their public spheres are restricted to the places their parents believe are safe, their thoughts are filled with religious pieties which are designed to direct their eyes away from injustice, their air is purified only in their household, their neighborhood is segregated by class and race, and their daily activities are gendered, whether at school or home. Their father hopes to preserve their childhood in an ideal sense by having them overlook symptoms of social problems and to ignore causes altogether. Bennett's sense of childhood is a social construction of his privilege, in which impulse and empathy are designed to protect his position. The impulses he hopes to control include the ones in which people attempt to right injustices when the law (and those enforcing it) are determined to keep the status quo. The empathy he intends to extend does not require the morally literate to consider the oppression of others. Compare Bennett's notion of childhood with those which Juan Gonzales (1995), Jim Hubbard, (1996), and Jonathan Kozol (2000) present. Not everyone lives in Chevy Chase, Maryland (where the Bennetts lived when *The Book of Virtues* was written), and not even everyone in Chevy Chase experiences Bennett's childhood.

The stories at the beginning of the chapter suggest that morals do matter, but they point us in a different direction than the one that Bennett and others try to sell us (Shannon, 2000a). Let us begin by recognizing that fixed moral positions do not serve to explain the complexity of lives involved in these stories. We can develop reasoned positions to account for the actions of all the agents within them. (I'll admit that I have trouble accepting some of these positions, but I do not dispute the possible sincerity of those who develop them.) Those reasoned positions certainly pose problems for the people involved, and they also pose problems for democratic life when some of them are afforded more power than others to determine what actions might or might not be taken. In each of these stories, power was distributed unequally, leading to questionable moral actions, and then, a biased airing of the reasoned positions in the media in order to explain them. Bennett's moral literacy is designed to ignore power relationships. In fact, Bennett's moral and commercial pedagogues explicitly seek to disable readers' abilities to consider power relationships at all. To paraphrase Sonny Boy Williamson, Bennett hopes to fatten us up to be eaten by a new power elite.

In order to consider these and other stories carefully, we need a different type of moral literacy—one that considers both the plurality of positions and fundamentals of democracy (Shannon, 2000b). Bennett is correct that twentieth-century attempts at democracy have failed. He is wrong, however, that increased recognition of diversity has caused these failures. Rather these failures are predictable based on the inabilities of conservatives, liberals, and even collectivists to take up issues of diversity productively (Trend, 1996). "What we share and what makes us fellow citizens in a liberal democratic regime is not a substantive idea of the good, but a set of political principles specific to such a tradition: the principles of freedom and equality for all" (Mouffee, 1993, p. 65). Although conservatives and liberals claim their positions to be founded on these principles, their visions of "the good" require them to demand consensus around their positions. Bennett is clear that he wants us to habituate his position of freedom and equality. Yet, democratic politics require adversarial relations among social actors as they advocate their interpretations and their preferred social identities.

> It is the tension between consensus—on the values—and dissensus—on the interpretation—that makes possible the agnostic dynamics of pluralist democracy. This is why its survival depends on the possibility of forming

collective political identities around clearly differentiated positions and the choice among real alternatives (Mouffee, 1995, p. 107).

For democracy to work, individuals must recognize that their identities are not fixed, abstract, or universal as Bennett maintains. Rather our identities are multiple and fluid. We are members of many social groups that influence our thoughts, actions, and values in substantial ways, and we vary our hierarchical arrangements of those memberships according to circumstances and intentions. Beyond that recognition, citizens must learn to use their moral power to force clear articulations of positions by forming coalitions to enact their shared concerns (Stone, 1994). Moral literacy can and should play an important role in providing this force. Democracy, then, hinges on the development of individuals' identities that are committed to the value of freedom and equality (blended with the values of their other group memberships), to moral literacies focused on clear articulations of alternatives, and to active participation in civic life. Although these identities cannot be fully specified, they require at least three elements: reflexive agency, the will to act, and respect for the positions of adversaries.

Reflexive agency invites citizens to evaluate the world in terms of their intentions and values, and at the same time, to evaluate those intentions and to reflect on those values. In this way citizens take inventory of their identities, their values, their motives and their actions, they investigate the sources of those parts of themselves, and they make choices about which ones they hope to enhance and which they hope to diminish. Compare this agency with Bennett's notion that meanings are static, allowing standard reading of texts across time and space. Consider how this agency undermines the authority hidden in Bennett's commercial packaging.

The will to act, which for many has been diverted from public life to private matters of consumption (Schor, 2000), must be redirected through individuals' recognition that their apparently private problems are connected to public issues because the problem is shared by many. As individuals become aware of the political possibilities of their multiple and fluid identities and the real opportunities to form larger, more effective coalitions for accomplishing goals shared across social groups, the will to act in civic life increases in likelihood. Bennett considers morality a solely individual concern—all persons responsible completely for their actions and the consequences. Collective moral action is out of the question. Recognizing that personal problems are often public issues invites consideration of institutional morality and the will to act collectively on those considerations. Reflexive agency ensures that coalitions will not become fixed power blocks as basic and secondary assumptions for action are consistently scrutinized.

Because our identities are not fixed and future intersections of values cannot be predetermined, citizens begin to recognize the need to respect the positions of their adversaries—not to the point of agreement, mind you—but enough to recognize commitment to shared principles of freedom and equality. Perhaps this is how Ralph Nader and Phyllis Schlafly can find common ground on commercial exploitation of children in schools. The limits on this respect must be set by individuals' and groups' commitments to those principles. Anyone rejecting freedom and equality outright stands outside of the democratic process and, therefore, becomes the legitimate object of democratic scorn.

The social problems we face and the demands of democracy require more than Bennett or any of the other moral entrepreneurs can package and sell to us. Different moral literacies—ones based on reflexive agency, a will to act, and respect for adversaries' positions—will not automatically solve the moral issues facing us. They will not make it easy for children or adults to choose moral courses of action. They will, however, prepare us to look beneath the surface of the particulars of our concerns. They will enable us to see that our problems are not ours alone. They will help us to listen seriously to the moral positions put forth by others. They will help us to understand the conflict that arises out of these various positions and to seek coalition with those others who seem to share a common goal with us on those concerns. They will help us understand how power works and to use our collective strengths to identify and maintain structures that will extend freedom and equality into more aspects of our lives.

# References

Bennett, W. (1984). *To Reclaim a Legacy.* Washington, DC: National Endowment for the Humanities.

Bennett, W. (1988). *Our Children and Our Country.* New York: Simon and Schuster.

Bennett, W. (1992). *The De-Valuing of America.* New York: Simon and Schuster.

Bennett, W. (1993). *The Book of Virtues: A Treasury of Great Moral Stories.* New York: Simon and Schuster.

Bennett, W. (1994). *The Index of Cultural Indicators.* New York: Broadway Books.

Bennett, W. (1995). *The Children's Book Of Virtue.* New York: Simon and Schuster.

Bennett, W. (1996). *Adventures From The Book of Virtues.* New York: Simon and Schuster.

Bennett, W. (1996). *Body Count.* New York: Simon and Schuster.

Bennett, W. (1996). *The Moral Compass.* New York: Touchstone.

Bennett, W. (1997). *The Book of Virtues For Young People.* New York: Simon and Schuster.

Bennett, W. (1997). *The Children's Book of Heroes.* New York: Simon and Schuster.

Bennett, W. (1997). *Our Sacred Honor.* New York: Broaden and Holman.

Bennett, W. (1998) *The Children's Book of America.* New York: Simon and Schuster.

Bennett, W. (1998). *The Death of Outrage: Bill Clinton and the Assault on American Ideals.* New York: Free Press.

Bennett, W. (1998). *Our Country's Founders.* New York: Simon and Schuster.

Bennett, W. (1998). *The Spirit of America.* New York: Touchstone.

Bennett, W. (1999). *The Index of Leading Cultural Indicators.* Colorado Springs: Waterbrook Press.

Bennett, W., with Finn, C. & Cribb, J. (1999). *The Educated Child.* New York: Free Press.

Black Panther Party Platform. (1966). In J. Albert & S. Albert (eds.), *The Sixties Papers.* New York: Praeger.

Bourdieu, P. (1984). *Distinction.* New York: Routledge.

Cherryholmes, C. (1999). *Reading Pragmatism.* New York: Routledge.

Foucault, M. (1972). *The Archeology Of Knowledge.* London: Tavistock.

Fraser, N. (1997). *Justice interruptus.* New York: Routledge.

Gee, J. (1992). What is literacy?. In P. Shannon (ed.), *Becoming Political.* Portsmouth, NH: Heinemann.

Gonzales, J. (1995). *Roll up your windows*. New York: Verso.

Greider, W. (1998). *One World, Ready Or Not*. New York: Touchstone.

Hall, S. (1992). The West And The Rest. In S. Hall & B. Gieben (eds.), *Foundations of Modernity*. Cambridge, UK: Open University Press.

Heilbronner, R. (1985). *The Nature and Logic of Capitalism*. New York: Norton.

Hooks, b. (1989). *Talking Back*. Boston: South End Press.

Hubbard, J. (1996). *Their Lives Turned Upside Down*. New York: Simon & Schuster.

Kitman, J. (2000, March 20). The Secret History of Lead. *The Nation*, 270, 11, pp. 11-24.

Kozol, J. (2000). *Ordinary Resurrections*. New York: Crown.

Lear, J. (1994) *Fables Of Abundance*. New York: Basic Books.

Marcuse, H. (1993). *One Dimensional Man*. Boston: Beacon.

Marx, K. (1967). *Capital*, vol. 1. New York: International Press.

Mouffee, C. (1993). *The Return Of The Political*. New York: Verso.

Mouffee, C. (1995). Politics, Democratic Action, And Solidarity. *Inquiry*, 38 (pp. 99–108).

Nash, R. (1997). *Answering The Virtuecrats*. New York: Teachers College Press.

Putnam, R. (2000). *Bowling Alone*. New York: Simon & Schuster.

Redstocking Manifesto. (1969). In J. Alpert & S. Alpert (eds.). *The sixties papers*. New York: Praeger.

Schor, J. (2000). *Do Americans Shop Too Much?* Boston: Beacon.

Shannon, P. (2000a). What's My Name. *Reading Research Quarterly*. 35 (pp. 90–108).

Shannon, P. (2000b). *You'd Better Shop Around*. Portsmouth, NH: Heinemann.

Sklar, H. (1995) *Chaos or Community?* Boston: South End Press.

SNCC Speaks for Itself. (1965). In J. Alpert & S. Alpert (eds.), *The Sixties Papers*. New York: Praeger.

Stone, J. (1994). The Phenomenological Roots Of The Radical Democracy/Marxism Debate. *Rethinking Marxism*, 7 (pp. 99–115).

Trend, D. (ed.) (1996). *Radical Democracy*. New York: Routledge.

Welch, S. (1985). *Communities Of Resistance And Solidarity*. New York: Orbis.

West, C. (1993). *Race Matters*. Boston: Beacon Press.

Widemann, J. (1995). Doing Time, Marking Race. *Nation* (30 October) (pp. 502–503).

Wollstonecraft, M. (1792). *A Vindication of the Rights of Women: With Strictures on Political and Moral Subjects*. Boston: Thomas & Andrews.

# Chapter Seven

## Smoke and Mirrors: Language Policy and Educational Reform

*Kris D. Gutierrez*

It is easy to identify and criticize the American school preoccupation with failure, for the evidence is abundant that too many people leave school scarred. The more difficult task is to come to a point where one can think about education and schooling without thinking about failure or success as categories for the identification of children (Varenne & McDermott, 1999, p. xi).

In their recent book *Successful Failure: The School America Builds*, Varenne and McDermott expose American schools' preoccupation with talking about and responding to children in terms of the categories that schools have constructed for them. They call for a dismantling of the language of success and failure and for building a new language for the way we think and go about educating our nation's children. I can think of no more urgent time to challenge the current language and practices of education, as the related discourses of educational reform and anti-immigrant agenda are an inherent part of our current schooling practices.

California today is a rich case study of how the language of success and failure is encoded in educational and social reform agenda. Couched in the rhetoric of progress, accountability, and higher standards, the reforms are ostensibly about the achievement or underachievement of minority students, particularly Latino, and all the reforms are aimed toward fixing Latino and other language minority students. Sustained by a nostalgia for the golden age of entitlement and privilege that existed before the incremental changes of the civil rights movement and rapidly changing state demographics, the discourse of reform in California has become a reactionary response to diversity and difference (Gutierrez, Asato, Santos, & Gotanda, in press). Thus, despite the legal and political rhetorical maneuvering, educational reform in California is necessarily about normalizing large numbers of linguistically and culturally diverse children and the social and cultural practices in which they engage; it is also about normalizing their educational practices, and the educators who must implement them (Gutierrez, Baquedano-Lopez, & Alvarez, 2000).

In this chapter I will discuss how anti-immigrant and educational reform policies have come together to bolster the large-scale implementation of new language and literacy practices in the state. I hope to demonstrate the insidious means by which failure is continually reproduced for an extremely vulnerable population: the English-language learner; and to expose that the underachievement and academic failure of Latino children is becoming the accepted norm. In doing so, I will illustrate how a recent language policy becomes the vehicle for socializing large numbers of people toward a new language ideology (or maybe it's not so new), as well as the rationale for sorting children into categories and curricular programs.

## Smoke and Mirrors

The conditions for the predictable failure of vulnerable student populations are in place. Consider the current struggles in our state where the incremental gains of the civil rights movement have been lost. In the past decade, voters in California have proposed the elimination of health and educational services for undocumented immigrants (Proposition 187)[2] and overturned affirmative action (Proposition 209). At the same time, university regents limited access for historically marginalized student populations by eliminating race as one criterion for admission to the University of California, the premier system of higher education in the state (SP1). The anti-immigrant and anti-affirmative action sentiments of Propositions 187, 209, and SP1 were reinforced further by Proposition 227, a measure that essentially eliminated bilingual education by restricting the use of the primary language in instructional contexts and mandating English-only instruction for all English language learners.

In this particular context, the operant backlash politics are largely a reactionary response to the dramatic shift in the demographics of California and in its public schools. The extraordinary numbers of English-language learners, predominantly Latino, have created a new educational challenge that has been met with resistance from educators, politicians, and the general populace. The collective response this time, however, has become more pernicious, exclusionary, and more overtly

---

[2]Proposition 187, which targeted the state's immigrant population, would have made it illegal for immigrants to use health, education, and social services. This measure would have required teachers/schools to report undocumented children or children of undocumented immigrants to authorities. The Proposition was deemed unconstitutional and was not implemented. Nevertheless, the foundation for anti-immigrant sentiment was set.

racialized. This primarily anti-Latino immigrant reform package effectively employed a language of reform that both devalued the Spanish language (and other native languages), its utility, and thus, its community. Language use, then, has become the centerpiece of the educational reform agenda, and has had particular consequences for linguistic minorities (Gutierrez, Asato, Santos, & Gotanda, in press).[3]

If we accept Ochs' (1988, 1992) premise that language has a powerful role in indexing and shaping ideologies, then we begin to understand the particular role that this language of reform can have on shaping racialized ideologies and giving meaning to the social and cultural practices of the racialized group, including its potential educational successes and failures. By reframing an old English-only policy as an educational reform designed to increase student achievement, *English for the Children*, as the refurbished policy was packaged, not only privileged English but also made it the solution to the educational problems of urban schools. The new discourse has made it acceptable to express what in previous eras might have been considered taboo. Consider one practicing elementary school teacher's reactions to the new language policy in her district:

> Um. I have to tell you I really disagreed with bilingual education. It was something I did not want to do. I think it probably cost me my first job. Not cost me, but the principal wanted me to…was really big on it. And I was not. You know, you're in this country, learn the language. You have that second language, good for you. It's a public school, and you know, you're here to learn English. I do not think we should be teaching you a language that's not English. If you want to pick it up at home, hey that's great, there's Saturday school, there's Sunday school. Pick it up at home with your parents. Um. You know. If you need me to translate something for you. I'm more than happy to do it. But I do not agree with giving you the same book that the kids have in English in Spanish and facilitating that. If you already know how to read, here's a Spanish book, read it in Spanish. If you do not know how to read, I'm not going to sit here and teach you how to read in Spanish. If I do not even know how to teach you to read in English, how am I going to do it in another language? (Interview, Ms. Contreras, November 13, 1998).

The critique here is not about political correctness; instead, this teacher's beliefs, like so much of public discourse, reflects on a historical understanding of the language policies and practices that English-language learners have experienced over our nation's history, or even the past four decades. As we have argued in previous work, before there was bilingual education, there was English immersion (Gutierrez, Asato,

---

[3] See our work, *Backlash Pedagogy*, for a fuller discussion of this backlash and its pedagogical and social consequences.

Santos, & Gotanda, in press). Thus, while these reforms are put forth as advances, they are consciously historical in their conceptualizations.

In 1974, *Lau v. Nichols* provided the legal remedy that mandated that English-language learners receive the same instruction as English-speaking children (*Lau v. Nichols*, 414 U.S. 563,1974). As the Supreme Court argued three decades ago:

> There is no equality of treatment merely by providing students with the same facilities, textbooks, teachers, and curriculum; for students who do not understand English are effectively foreclosed from any meaningful education.

Instruction in the students' home language was one robust remedy identified in response to the decision. The new language policy, undergirded by a xenophobic ideology, ignores the historical conditions that mandated a legal remedy. Of significance, the *English for the Children* policy legislates more than English as the language of instruction; it essentially limits equal opportunities to learn, as the following account from one local teacher illustrates:

> Okay, ooh. I think I understand this correctly. The law is that um. myself, I am not allowed to use the second language in the classroom. Any facilitating of the second language needs to be through my aide. She is to work with the kids is what my understanding is. And that's kind of pretty much how I do it. But it makes no sense to me. And last year, my aide was not allowed to do instruction to the bilingual kids. You know, it had to be me, even though I didn't have my BCLAD. And, you know, I'm working on my CLAD.[4] But you know, either way. I was qualified to teach a Spanish class, but I was able to do this. But you know, I had to do it to my Spanish kids. And now, I have to have a bilingual aide. And I'm not allowed to work with the kids. It has to be the aide giving instruction to the kids which to me makes no sense. You know I'd rather have my aide work with the kids that understand. And let me facilitate because I'm the one who went to school. I'm the one who's still going to school for my CLAD. I'm the one who knows the background or how they acquire a language and all those things. I'm the one who's more prepared. So why can't I do it. But I feel bad sometimes, because the kids tell me, "Ms. Lopez, why do not you ever read with us?" And it's like, well, I'll still read with you, but I never get to it. Cuz, my aide is reading with them. You know, I have four other groups to read with, three others and I do not...I can't get to them. I can't. (Interview, Ms. Lopez, 6th grade teacher, November, 13, 1998.)

Ms. Lopez's frustration is echoed by so many well-trained,

---

[4] Teachers in California can earn several certificates that prepare them for teaching diverse student  populations. The BCLAD, Bilingual Crosscultural Language and Academic Development, certifies that the teacher is trained to teach in the students' primary language; the CLAD certificate, Crosscultural Language and Academic Development,  permits the teacher to teach in classrooms designated for English-language learners.

experienced teachers who are unable to use their knowledge to assist their students' learning. Teachers participating in highly prescriptive English reading programs throughout the state report the various ways their expertise and experience in teaching literacy is thwarted by the hyper-regulation of new reading approaches. In one particular school in California, a teacher was reprimanded by his principal for supplementing the curriculum with trade books that he had previously used with success:

*Memorandum*

*TO:          (teacher's name)*
*FROM:      (principal's name & title)*
*SUBJECT   Classroom visit*

> *During my visit to your classroom this morning I noticed many supplemental books from either [names specific materials] or other materials maybe from your reading recovery stock. I asked you when these books are used and you said that you teach with Open Court and use these other books also.*
>
> *It is very important to utilize only the Open Court materials during the prescribed reading time and no other trade books during the directed teacher lessons except for those books that Open Court recommends to complement the modules. It is obvious that you continue to do your own program. It is insubordinate [sic] to refuse to implement the Open Court reading program as prescribed.*
>
> *Your training in the area of reading is extensive and I respect your need to utilize your training but in lieu of the fact that we are an Open Court school, mandatory that the script be followed.*
>
> *Thank you for your immediate compliance to this direction.* (personal communication, 1999).

Such highly scripted and regulated programs strip teachers of their agency and expertise; this deskilling of teachers further serves to normalize teachers and their teaching practices toward a new language ideology. Of significance for English-language learning communities: the decontextualization of teaching from the respective learning community makes it easier to rationalize the prohibition of the students' home language in the acquisition of literacy and content knowledge.

Even in classrooms that permit limited use of the primary language in whole class instruction, teachers are not allowed to use Spanish, for example, to assist Spanish-speaking children who require help as they work independently:

> [The children ] are creating a book with eight pages about a specific
> animal. Each page has questions and the students must write three facts in
> response to each question. The Spanish readers do their books in Spanish. [The
> teacher] reminded [Graciela, a first grade child] that her primary language is
> Spanish and that her book must be in Spanish, not English. This is independent
> work so the teachers are not offering assistance.(fieldnote, 2/9/99, pp. 133–
> 136).

Relegated to the tutelage of sincere but less-trained and experienced
aides, those children most in need of expert assistance in an English-only
context are denied access to the same instructional support English-
speaking children receive. The irony is not lost here. Prohibited from
using the children's primary language, teachers in English immersion
programs also may no longer use primary language materials to mediate
students' learning of language and content. Although the new law does
not prevent the use of such materials in modified or structured immersion
programs, many school districts literally threw out all available primary
language materials immediately. In the months after the passage of
Proposition 227, I personally observed new and old Spanish language
textbooks, reading materials, trade books, and other support materials
piled up in hallways, storage rooms, in trash dumpsters, and classroom
corners. As one teacher observed:

> …I mean all the books and stuff they bought. It's all virtually sitting in my
> classroom collecting dust. I can send it home with them if they select it, but I
> can't direct them to the books. And another thing that happened because of the
> Proposition is that now there aren't enough social studies books. They bought
> all these Spanish books, but now there aren't enough English books in the
> district. So they can't even take the books home for homework! (Interview,
> Ms. Smith, 5th grade teacher, November 4, 1998).

The rush to replace Spanish and other home languages came at the
expense of deep learning and literacy development. Developing oral
English skills rather than becoming literate and biliterate became the
focus of instruction:

> I (research assistant) ask [the teacher] how it has been going. She says,
> "it's okay." She shrugs her shoulders before continuing. "Some were crying
> because it was the first time they had seen something all in English. But this
> year, they're mentally ready." She smiles and lowers her voice, covering her
> mouth as if making a confession. But the skills are not ready." (fieldnote
> 5/11/99).

Yet another teacher notes the increased vocabulary development
among the  English-language learners at the expense of comprehension:

...this is especially true especially for Mrs. Hanover's kids because Mrs. Hanover doesn't use any Spanish. Lots of kids can decode very well, but understanding is another story. (field note, 1/26/99).

This emphasis on oral English language development was accompanied by statewide reading reforms that required dramatic changes in content and pedagogy in all English language arts programs. Moreover, in a push to increase reading achievement in the early grades, English-language learners were immersed in district mandated and state-supported reading programs developed for English dominant students. Once again, the conditions that construct the underachievement of the most vulnerable student population were firmly put in place. Even if we could accept the premise that such programs could be applicable to English-language learners, our research suggests that such reductive literacy practices, i.e., an exclusive focus on the acquisition of phonemic awareness and phonemic skills, excludes these students from the opportunity to develop a larger repertoire of meaning-making skills essential to reading comprehension and interpretation. The reductive literacy approaches ignore the consistent research findings that emergent readers (read print in familiar language better than they do unfamiliar print) (Coles, 2000).

This one size fits all approach denies the heterogeneity that exists among all children, including English-language learners, and excludes the rich sociocultural and linguistic experiences that all children can bring to learning tasks (Gutierrez, Baquedano-Lopez, Alvarez, & Chiu, 1999; Gutierrez, Baquedano-Lopez, & Turner, 1997). The narrow conceptualization of literacy further underscores the language ideology of the *English for the Children* policy. Language, the most powerful mediating tool, in this case the children's primary language, is excluded from the students' learning toolkit. Our long-term ethnographic research in urban schools belies this new orientation. In particular, our work on effective literacy practices for English-language learners has highlighted the necessary and sufficient conditions that help ensure robust learning for linguistically diverse learning populations. In effect, we can say with confidence that robust learning communities share several common features. In general, these effective learning communities:

• mediate learning or assist learning in a variety of ways; in cultural-historical terms, we say that rich learning communities use multiple mediational tools;
• employ heterogeneity and hybridity as organizing principles of instruction, including hybrid language practices;
• utilize all the social, cultural, and linguistic resources of all participants;

- regard diversity and difference as resources for learning; and
- define learning rather than teaching as the targeted goal  (Gutierrez, 2000).

Such rich learning communities challenge the normalizing baseline of the English-only practices, including their underlying ideologies. Fundamentally, these new reductive literacy practices do not harness diversity and difference as resources for learning;  instead, these new pedagogies are characterized by reductive notions of learning, particularly literacy and language learning, that define diversity and difference as problems to be eliminated or remediated. Thus, the new literacy necessarily prohibits the use of students' complete linguistic, sociocultural, and academic repertoire in the service of learning. In this way, the *English for the Children* policy, and its accompanying literacy practices,  institutionalize the conditions for underachievement and school failure with no consideration of the sociohistorical context of racism and classism in this country and its manifestation in educational policies, practices, and outcomes.

Although the consequences of these new literacy practices on English only students of color is not the stated focus of this chapter, these policies have significant consequences for all urban children whose dialects and registers are both devalued and excluded:

> I was struck by the silence when I entered the classroom. The teacher, positioned at the front of the traditionally organized room, began to speak. "Where's the adjective in this sentence?" A third grade African-American girl eagerly raised her hand and spoke, "The adjective in this sentence is red and it's an adjective because it...." You could almost hear the gasp from the adults visiting the class with me. My conversations with them later confirmed what I thought they were thinking. Grammar still mystified them and they were impressed. Moreover, it was not so much the grammatical knowledge the child had displayed but the perfect standard English she employed to answer the teacher's question. Never mind that the children responded according to the script that had been prescribed for them. It seemed that in one swoop, the children were appropriating some skills and the register of the academy. Later as I observed one Latina child working diligently on providing the missing words for a story the students were asked to write. She had indeed filled in all the missing words correctly. I crouched next to her and asked her to tell me about her story. She read verbatim what she had written on her page. I then asked her in Spanish to tell me what her story was about. She explained in a whisper that she couldn't tell me because she didn't know what the story was about. She had learned to follow the prompts and that made her look successful, but she hadn't understood the text (fieldnote, 06/18/00).

The New Literacy in California is a robust example of the social construction of failure. In particular, the combination of reductive literacy practices and English-only policies help sustain the achievement gap between rich and poor, especially the poor language minority child. The New Literacy helps to coconstruct school identities that categorize and sort children in ways that undermine their competence and confidence.

We documented the trauma and confusion so many children experienced as they shifted from bilingual to monolingual instruction thirty days into the new school year.[5] Thrust into an unfamiliar context, the children expressed their fear of failure and fitting in an English-only learning context. "I was sad," said Bobby. "It felt like I didn't know everybody. I was sad. I felt like I didn't know anything." Although excited about her new move to an English-only class, Alma was intimidated by her new peers. "I thought I couldn't make any friends with Mrs. Hanover's class because they all speak English" (field note, 6/24/99).

During the first few months of post 227 instruction, children were often confused about what language they were required to use or which program they were in:

> Ms. Rocha says, "if you're in Spanish only, answer Spanish questions and write your words in Spanish. ...A student asks, "Spanish or English?" The teacher responds, "odd chapter, English." The students then ask, "If you're in Spanish language do you do it in Spanish?" "You have the option," responds the teacher. "Some of you, from reading your essays, I know you are capable. If you're not very proficient, still not confident, do it in Spanish. Transition [students in a transition to English program], you have no choice; you just do it in English." (fieldnote 10/22/98, pp. 3, 8–13).

In yet another classroom, the teacher reminds the newly designated English language readers where they needed to go for morning instruction.

> One student, Carlos, raises his hand and asks, "Where do I go teacher?" She looks at him and says, "No, Carlos, you stay here. You're a Spanish reader." (fieldnote, 01/26/99, pp. 2, 12–16).

Finally, these policies and practices have created a culture of fear and mistrust in schools. Children were often concerned about the legal

---

[5] This research is a collective effort that includes two Ph.D. students. These data were collected primarily by the research assistants Jolynn Asato and Anita Revilla for our study of *The Effects of Proposition 227 on the Teaching and Learning of English Language Learners*. Their work and insight must be acknowledged here.

sanctions their teachers would face if they spoke Spanish. "But you're not supposed to [speak Spanish] cuz it's against the law," was a refrain frequently heard in the classrooms. The children and teachers' fears were not unfounded. Indeed, the law had written in provisions for teachers to be sued if they were out of compliance with the new policy. Yet, the ambiguity in the policy made it subject to multiple interpretations. Consequently, there was a hyperinterpretation of the law among school and district personnel, as well as in the community. In one meeting with elementary school teachers, for example, teachers reported their understanding of the law:

| | |
|---|---|
| Jane: | Everything that goes home is supposed to be in English. |
| Researcher: | And where did that interpretation come from? |
| Jane: | Who knows? |
| Teacher 1: | I do not know. |
| Teacher 2: | I do not know. |
| Jane: | Well it's just… |
| Teacher 3: | Well I think from the law itself, the way it's written, that parents now have the luxury of suing a teacher, um, if the teacher is sending work home in Spanish. So I mean I have some math books that are in Spanish, but yet if I, when I send homework, I have one version in English, one. And I run copies off from there to send for homework. Because I always have that in the back of my mind, will a parent take this opportunity to sue me or the district or you know, because I'm sending something home in Spanish (fieldnote, 5/7/99). |

What are the consequences for the teaching and learning of literacy when teachers and students are monitored, hyperregulated, and restricted to a narrow set of beliefs and practices? Our work presents some hope. If our goal is to help all students make meaning and learn from their interactions and participation in various communities, we need to understand that language instruction should provide students with frequent opportunities both to use and develop an expansive repertoire of literacy skills and behaviors. Through participation in robust and respectful learning communities, students can develop a toolkit, that is, a set of linguistic, cognitive, and sociocultural tools and practices, that enhances learning. This toolkit reflects one's linguistic, sociocultural, and institutional identities—past, present, and potential. Not all theories and ways of organizing learning permit and promote the use of an individual's toolkit in the service of learning. Teacher preparation programs must examine their current constellation of practices and the theories of learning that underpin these practices. How English/language arts and teacher educators conceptualize teaching and learning in the twenty-first century remains an empirical question. I am optimistic that we will adopt robust theories of learning that ensure academic achievement  and democratic citizenship for all of our students.

# References

Coles, G. (2000). *Misreading Reading: The Bad Science That Hurts Children.* Portsmouth, NH: Heinemann Press.

Gutierrez, K. (2000). Teaching and learning in the 21st Century. *English Education, 32* (4), (pp. 290–299).

Gutierrez, K., Asato, J., Santos, M., & Gotanda, N. (in press). Backlash Pedagogy: Language and Culture and the Politics of Reform. In M. Suarez-Orozco (Ed.), *Latinos in the 21st Century.* Berkeley: University of California Press.

Gutierrez, K., Baquedano-Lopez, P., Alvarez, H, & Chiu, M. (1999). A cultural-historical approach to collaboration: Building a culture of collaboration through hybrid language practices. *Theory into Practice, 38* (2). (pp. 87–93).

Gutierrez, K., Baquedano-Lopez, P., & Alvarez, H. (2000). The crisis in Latino education: Challenging the current debate. In C. Tejeda, C. Martinez, & Z. Leonardo (Eds.), *Demarcating the borders of Chicana(o)/Latina(o) education.* Cresskill, NJ: Hampton Press Inc.

Gutierrez, K., Baquedano-Lopez, P., & Tejeda, C. (2000). Rethinking Diversity: Hybridity and Hybrid Language Practices in the Third Space. *Mind, Culture, and Activity, 6* (4). (pp. 286–303).

Gutierrez, K., Baquedano-Lopez, P., & Turner, M. G. (1997). Putting language back into language arts: When the radical middle meets the third space. *Language Arts, 74* (5). (pp. 368–378).

Ochs, E. (1992). Indexing gender. In A. Duranti & C. Goodwin (Eds),. *Rethinking context: Language as an interactive phenomenon.* New York: Cambridge University Press. (pp. 335–358).

Ochs, E. (1988). *Language Socialization.* New York: Cambridge University Press.

Varenne, H., & McDermott, R. (1999). *Successful Failure: The School America Builds.* Boulder, CO: Westview Press.

## Chapter Eight

# Look, the Emperor Has No Clothes: An Educator's Guide to Choosing Cost-Effective Literacy Programs

*Brian O. Brent*

## Overview

According to a classic fairy tale, a merchant can make an emperor parade around in the nude if he can persuade him that he is wearing elegant, but invisible, clothes. The moral of the fable, of course, is that if people do not want to waste money, to say nothing of looking foolish, they must consider carefully the merits and costs of the items that they purchase. As stressed often in this book, teachers and administrators must all make choices. For instance, an administrator might choose between whole language and phonics instruction or between Reading Recovery and Success for All Schools. Similarly, a teacher could choose any one of a hundred big books to teach reading skills. The purpose of this chapter is not to champion or oppose any of these instructional approaches to literacy. Instead, the central task of this chapter is to introduce an analytical framework that will enable teachers and administrators to balance for themselves the merits and costs of alternative literacy programs.[6] Put simply, the emphasis here is not on *what* to decide, but *how* to decide.

The chapter begins by documenting policymakers' growing interest in the costs and effects of literacy programs. I give particular attention to the emergence of high-stakes accountability systems and note the pressure placed on teachers and administrators to demonstrate that their program choices are "cost-effective." Next, I argue that educators should embrace, not fear, discussion of cost-effectiveness. This discussion sets the stage for the remainder of the chapter. Here I provide an understanding of cost-effective analysis in a decision-oriented frame-work. My hope is that an introduction to cost-effectiveness analysis might encourage and enable teachers and administrators to incorporate this approach into their evaluation of literacy programs. In addition, educators can also use cost-effectiveness analysis to gain much needed

---

[6] I use the term literacy program to describe any philosophy, approach, technology, or product that facilitates literacy instruction.

political support for their efforts to improve student literacy.

## Why Consider Cost and Effects?

In recent years, public attention has shifted away from concerns about student equity to concerns about how well students are performing relative to costs. For example, most state and local policymakers embrace the notion of standards-based accountability (Ladd & Hansen, 1996). In general, standards-based accountability means that students must attain some standard of competency, and schools must devise methods of relating expenditures to student achievement levels. Put simply, policymakers are now comparing costs and results, and holding teachers and administrators accountable for them.

Standards-based accountability systems emerged for several reasons. First, fueled by international comparisons of student achievement, policymakers feared that the United States was losing its economic advantage. To right the course, policymakers called for higher academic standards and new assessment systems (Allington & Woodside-Jiron, 1999; Gratz, 2000). Although a national standards movement faltered, state legislators answered the call. Most states now hold schools accountable for student performance through an array of monitoring and sanctioning tactics that include school report cards, providing bonuses to high-performing schools, and placing struggling schools on watch lists. Some states have even enacted laws that permit the replacement of administrators and teachers if students do not meet academic standards (Malen & Muncey, 2000). To be sure, these are high-stakes accountability systems.

Secondly, calls for standards-based accountability were prompted by a series of blue ribbon reports that demonstrated that school spending has continued to rise dramatically while student performance has stagnated. For example, between 1970 and 1990, average inflation-adjusted per-pupil expenditures for public K-12 school rose more than 70 percent, while reading and writing scores on the National Assessment of Educational Progress remained stable (Walberg, 1996).[7] Despite the many plausible explanations for this phenomenon, such as the rising costs of special education, the public has come to doubt the standard nostrum of educational reformers that schools need more money. Instead, concerns that the public is not getting value for their money has pushed cost issues to the forefront of education policy debates.

---

[7] See also Chall (1996), Coulson (1996), and Stedman (1996).

Thirdly, standards-based accountability systems are drawing attention because policymakers expect that education dollars will be tight in the coming years. For example, K-12 enrollments are projected to increase 4 percent by 2009 (NCES, 1999). At the same time, the aging of the population will generate significant new demands for health care services. As long as economic growth remains constant, demands for new social services such as these will mean that fewer dollars are available for schools (Monk & King, 1993).

In summary, standards-based accountability systems pose a daunting challenge for teachers and administrators. Most states seem content to set achievement targets and leave curricular decisions to schools (Furhman, 1999). In these instances, there is intense pressure on teachers and administrators to demonstrate that their curricular choices produce the sought-after effects for the fewest dollars. When their choices fail to produce the promised results, policymakers and the public will want to know why.[8]

## What Is Cost-effectiveness Analysis?

It is desirable, in light of the growing concern over cost and student performance, to take stock of what cost-effectiveness analysis has to offer those concerned with the selection and implementation of literacy programs. Indeed, nearly all packaged literacy programs claim to be "cost-effective." However, a program is only cost-effective if it provides the best educational results for a given cost or provides a given level of educational results for the least cost. Stated more simply, those choosing a literacy program should ask two important questions:
1. Is there another literacy program that will provide better results for the same money?
2. Is there another literacy program that will provide the same results for less money?

Cost-effectiveness analysis can help educators answer these questions. Specifically, cost-effectiveness analysis facilitates the appraisal of alternative programs based on their costs *and* their effects in producing a desired outcome or set of outcomes.[9] A simple example can

---

[8] For a thoughtful discussion of the possibilities and perils of standards-based reform, see Ladd & Hansen (1996).

[9] Cost-effectiveness analysis is often confused with cost-benefit analysis. Although these decision-making tools are related, they differ in one important way. Cost-benefit analysis is appropriate only when the analyst can reasonably

help illustrate the concepts underlying this decision-making tool.

Suppose that your schoolboard asks you to select a literacy program for your school. Your first task is to specify the outcomes or objectives that you (or the board) want the program to produce.[10] For this example, assume that you want a program that will improve students' critical literacy.[11]

The second task is to identify a set of alternative programs that you believe will accomplish this objective. Let's assume that you find (or create) three programs, say, A, B, and C, that promise to improve critical literacy (see Figure 1).

**<u>Figure 1:</u>**

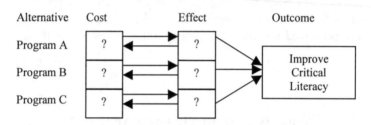

The third task is to consider the effects of each program. By definition, effects measure how well each program achieves the desired outcome; in this case, improving critical literacy. To keep our example simple, suppose that researchers can measure students' gain in critical

---

place a dollar value on the effects of a program. For example, a cost-benefit analysis of a program to stop smoking could express the effects of the program in terms of the dollars saved from reduced medical care for smoking-related illnesses. Expressing the effects of an educational program, however, is frequently more difficult. It would be nearly impossible, for example, to translate increases in student achievement or attitudes into monetary values. Consequently, cost-effectiveness analysis is more appropriate than cost-benefit analysis for most educational decisions. See Nas (1996) or Levin (1983) for further discussion of the appropriate uses of cost-benefit analysis.

[10] Cost-effectiveness analysis is only appropriate if the programs pursue the same goals. For example, cost-effectiveness analysis should not be used to compare the costs and effects of a mathematics program versus a literacy program. Nor, for that matter, should cost-effectiveness analysis be used to evaluate the merits of two literacy programs with markedly different goals, for instance, one focused on phonics and another focused on critical literacy.

[11] Anderson and Irvine (1993) define critical literacy as learning to read and write as part of the process of becoming conscious of one's experience as historically constructed within specific power relations. See Shor (2000) for a thoughtful discussion of principles and practices of critical literacy.

literacy using a "magical" test. In addition, assume that average gain scores for programs *A*, *B*, and *C* were 5, 25, and 30, respectively.

The fourth and final task is to determine the cost of each program (e.g., equipment, materials, and supplies). Typically, these figures are translated into a cost per student (i.e., total program cost divided by the number of students served). This allows the analysis to account for differences in the number of students served by each alternative program. In the present example, suppose that programs *A*, *B*, and *C* each serve twenty-five students and that the costs per student are $25, $50, and $90, respectively.

You now have the information needed to determine which program is most cost-effective. As can been seen in Table 1, Program C is the most effective, but it is also the most costly. On the other hand, Program A is the least costly, but it is also highly ineffective. Program B falls in the middle regarding both cost and effects.

**Table 1:**
**Cost-Effectiveness Data for Three Critical Literacy Programs**

| Program | Cost Per Student | Effectiveness (achievement gains) | Cost-Effectiveness Ratio |
|---|---|---|---|
| A | $25 | +5 points | $5:1 point |
| B | $50 | +25 points | $2:1 point |
| C | $90 | +30 points | $3:1 point |

To facilitate comparisons among these alternatives it is useful to calculate cost-effectiveness ratios. Cost-effectiveness ratios represent the cost to produce one unit of effects. For example, comparing the costs and effects of Program C yields a cost-effectiveness ratio of 3:1, indicating that its costs $3 to improve students' critical literacy by 1 point. Similarly, Program B yields a cost-effectiveness ratio of 2:1 and Program A yields a cost-effectiveness ratio of 5:1. The lower the ratio, the more cost-effective the alternative. Thus, Program B, with the lowest ratio, is the most cost-effective alternative.

To many, the identification of Program B as the most cost-effective alternative will hit a sour note. Indeed, most administrators and teachers want their students to have access to the most effective literacy programs available, regardless of cost. In fact, some may now believe that policymakers can use cost-effectiveness analysis to undermine the ability of schools to pursue important goals such as student learning. This view, however, indicates a fundamental misunderstanding of cost-effectiveness analysis as a decision-making tool.

Cost-effectiveness is not an educational goal in and of itself. Cost-effectiveness analysis merely provides information regarding which alternative achieves *your* desired outcome for the least cost. For example, if your goal were to increase critical literacy by an average of 30 points, Program C, the only program to produce the desired level of effects, would be the most cost-effective alternative. Stated simply, until the acceptable outcomes are established by the appropriate polity—students, teachers, administrators, community members, or policymakers, and, if possible, specified in some measurable way (e.g., achievement gains), cost-effectiveness has no meaning. Unfortunately, some mistakenly believe that the most cost-effective program is necessarily the least costly, regardless of effects. Our example indicates clearly that this is not the case.

In addition, cost-effectiveness analysis does not *dictate* decisions, but provides information to *inform* decisions. Even the strongest advocates of cost-effectiveness analysis acknowledge that there is no definitive choice. First, even in a well-conceived analysis, measures of the costs and effects of each alternative are typically estimates of those dimensions. This does not mean that they are biased or misleading, but they are always subject to some error. Secondly, it is never possible to include all of the considerations into an analysis that should inform the final decision. For example, organizational, social, or political factors might make one alternative easier to implement than another. Clearly, this information should be taken into account when considering which alternative to select.

The important point is that cost-effectiveness analysis is a decision-making tool. The decision maker should never use the results of the analysis such that the decision follows directly from the results. Rather, cost-effectiveness analysis provides information (albeit extremely important information) that must be combined with other pertinent data in selecting alternatives (Levin, 1983). Understood in this context, cost-effectiveness analysis is not something one needs to fear or oppose, it is simply a decision-making tool that enables educators to choose among alternative means to achieve their goal. This is no small advantage. The funds to support the overall educational program of a district are limited. Within any given budget, a decision to spend more on one program area will necessarily require a reduction in another area. Cost-effectiveness analysis helps administrators and teachers use available funds to provide the best program for students.

## Steps in Cost-Effectiveness Analysis

The case for using cost-effectiveness analysis to inform curricular decisions concerning literacy programs is compelling. Nevertheless, for many literacy teachers and administrators, the demands of cost-effectiveness analysis seem daunting. Not only are there calculations required, but a number of ambiguous terms guide the approach. In the remainder of this chapter, I will discuss how teachers and administrators can use cost-effectiveness analysis to inform decisions about the choice of literacy programs. The essence of my approach is simple: break the decision-making process into its key elements, specifying *outcomes*, identifying *alternatives*, and estimating *effects* and *costs;* apply some hard, systematic thinking, and make your decision.

### Specifying Outcomes (Objectives)

Too often, educators give short shrift to the outcomes that they want a literacy program to accomplish. In their impatience to choose a program, they plunge into other elements of the decision-making process without correctly identifying their objectives first. This is regrettable. The objectives you set guide the entire decision-making process, from defining alternatives at the outset, to analyzing those alternatives, to justifying the choice you ultimately make. Put simply, poorly defined objectives will lead to poor program choices.

Consider the following simple example. Suppose your board asks you to choose a new program to improve "student literacy." The objective, "to improve student literacy," however, is too ambiguous for decision-making purposes. In the first place, there is little consensus regarding what literacy entails. Some view literacy (or being literate) as a matter of word-formation, phonics, grammar, and comprehension skills. Others view literacy as a sociocultural practice in which reading and writing take place only within social, cultural, political, economic, and historical contexts (Gee, Hull, & Lankshear, 1996).[12]

Perhaps the board stated the objective in general terms as a means of securing consensus among stakeholders (e.g., parents, teachers, and administrators). Again, this is regrettable. Objectives need to be more than window dressing. Absent clarification of what it means to improve "literacy," your choice of program alternatives would be suspect. In fact, after some probing you may discover that your board was less interested

---

[12] For a useful discussion of the evolution of literacy principles and practices see de Castell and Luke (1983).

in improving literacy per se, and more interested in improving scores on state-administered reading exams.

Having noted the importance of defining program objectives clearly, I acknowledge that this can be a difficult task. However, you can make the task easier if you follow four steps:

Step 1: *Involve stakeholders in the objective-setting process.* Schools have many stakeholders and each may view the objective of a literacy program in radically different ways. For example, administrators may assert that the objective is to improve scores on state-administered exams, while teachers may assert that the objective is to develop critical literacy skills. Alternatively, parents might view the objective as encouraging lifelong reading habits. One way to improve the relevance of the analysis is to involve the various stakeholders in the objective setting process. This will not only ensure that important views have been registered, but will also increase subsequent commitment to the program (Alkin, Hofstetter, & Ai, 1998).

Step 2. *Create a comprehensive list of objectives.* Too often educators consider only a handful of objectives. There is also a tendency to focus on objectives whose attainment is easily measured (e.g., improving test scores) rather than those whose attainment is difficult to measure (e.g., create a classroom that models a democratic and just society) (Shannon, 1993; Stahl, 1999). In addition, most educators tend to stress short-term objectives (e.g., improving test scores) over long-term objectives (e.g., developing long-term cognitive processes or motivating children to become lifelong readers). A thorough cost-effectiveness analysis requires that *all* possible program objectives be identified and considered, even the difficult to measure.[13]

Step 3. *Define your objectives in ways that are clear and measurable.* Once you identify the list of objectives, you can then convert these objectives into succinct statements. The clearest and most easily communicated form for objectives is a short phrase consisting of a verb and an object, such as "improve student attitudes toward reading." The challenge here is to avoid ambiguity while not defining your objectives so narrowly that the analyses becomes unmanageable. For example, one could reasonably argue that an objective focused on improving students' attitude toward reading essays on say, colonial whaling, might be too narrowly defined. The broader your objective is, while still measurable, the more likely your analysis will be manageable and the results meaningful.[14]

Step 4. *Rank the objectives.* Some objectives may be complimentary,

---

[13] For more on identifying objectives see Nowakowski, (1985).

[14] See Popham (1999) for a thoughtful discussion on how to define objectives.

while others may be acquired only at the sacrifice of another. Where such objectives represent mutually exclusive program goals, one must be prepared to rank, in terms of preference, the various program objectives. For example, it might be decided that students' attitudes toward reading should be given twice the significance of standardized test scores. Moreover, it might be decided that creating a classroom that models a democratic society should be accorded equal weight to students' attitudes toward reading. Accordingly, you might decide on the weighting scheme presented in Table 2.

**Table 2:**
Illustrative Summary of Objective Preferences

| Objective | Weight |
| --- | --- |
| Improve Student Attitudes Toward Reading | 2 |
| Create a Classroom that Models a Democratic Society | 2 |
| Improve Standardized Test Scores | 1 |

Ranking objectives is a sufficiently difficult process when one considers only two competing goals and becomes increasingly more complex as additional objectives are considered. Nevertheless, teachers and administrators must be prepared to rank the multiple goals of instruction. The primary theme running through this discussion is that the decision-making process be systematic and as visible as possible. If you decide to place less emphasis on standardized test scores in favor of improving students' attitudes toward reading, this decision should be reflected openly. If there are those who wish to quarrel with the ranking, they may do so. The openness of such a process seems far more consonant with the premises of democracy and accountability than would be the case if educational objectives were selected behind closed doors in the superintendent's office.[15]

## Identifying Alternatives

Alternatives represent the range of potential choices you have for pursuing your objective, such as Programs A, B, and C in our previous example. Because of their central importance to the decision-making process, you should keep two points in mind at all times. First, it is important to place all pertinent alternatives on the agenda for consideration. This will require a comprehensive search for ways of

---

[15] For guidance on how to rank program objectives see Nagel and Bievenue (1993) and Edwards and Newman (1982).

meeting your objective. Although one may wish to draw upon traditional responses as well as those that other schools have used when facing similar situations, one should not be limited to these. In fact, often they might not be the most responsive alternatives.

For example, the traditional approach to literacy instruction has been to use commercial reading materials.[16] The explanation for this practice rests largely on teachers' and administrators' beliefs that commercial reading materials can teach children to read and that they are based on *current* research (Irvine & Larson, this volume) (Shannon, 1987). Curiously, it often takes between 15-20 years before publishers can translate research findings into commercial reading materials (see Anderson, Osborn, & Tierney, 1984). Consequently, reliance on these materials precludes teachers' implementing findings of the most recent research.[17]

Secondly, do not superficially evaluate alternatives while you are generating them. This will not only slow down the process but can result in the failure to consider potential alternatives. For example, one of the selling points of commercial reading materials is that they save teachers the time it would take to produce the materials themselves. Thus, given the heavy and increasing demands placed on teacher's time, it might seem reasonable to disregard the development of your own instructional materials. However, a perceived shortcoming should not keep you from listing the alternative. If some feature of the alternative is promising enough, it may be worth the effort to address the inadequacy later. Indeed, teachers that use commercial reading materials give up quite a bit to save time, including control over their instruction.

## Estimating Effects

Educators often use the terms outcome and effect interchangeably. While outcomes and effects are related, their specification requires two quite separate decisions. Outcomes refer to the goals or objectives of the program (i.e., what you hope to accomplish). Effects, on the other hand, are measures of whether an alternative has achieved your objective. Often, educators overlook this distinction when they become committed

---

[16] Commercial reading materials include readers, teacher's manuals, workbooks, worksheets, management components, and skills kits developed and produced by commercial publishing companies.

[17] See Shannon (1987) for a thoughtful discussion of the perils and possibilities of commercial reading materials.

to particular effectiveness measures. For example, many policymakers speak of test scores as if they are an objective. They are not. Test scores are one of many ways to measure whether a program has achieved an educational objective—student learning.

Consideration of the effects of different programs requires answers to two related questions: (a) w*hat* effects of the program should you estimate and, (b) having decided on what to estimate, *how* should you estimate these effects? The answer to the first question is straightforward. Unequivocally, your objectives determine what program effects you need to estimate. For instance, suppose your objective is to improve student attitudes toward reading. In this case, you would need to estimate how the different alternatives affect student attitudes. Again, the more clearly you state your objectives, the more useful they will be to you in answering the what-to-estimate question.

Once you have decided on what effects to estimate, the next step is to make the estimates. There are several ways one might approach this task. The first would be to refer to research studies that have examined the effects of your alternatives. This is often possible when one is choosing among so-called brand-name reform models that claim to be solutions for student literacy problems. For example, there is no shortage of studies that examine the effects of Success for All in meeting a number of objectives, including improving performance in reading and language arts and reducing grade-level retention and referrals to special education (e.g., Slavin, 1996; Venezky, 1998).

A second approach for estimating the effects of an alternative is to seek the counsel of a colleague, specifically one who uses the alternative to pursue the same objectives you specified. Too many classroom teachers carry out their professional responsibilities in isolation. If you want to know what people say will work, ask. In addition, there are a number of widely circulated practitioner periodicals that describe literacy programs that have demonstrated a variety of effects (e.g., X and Y).

A third approach is to examine reports from vendors or program developers regarding the alternatives. One, however, needs to view these reports with a bit of skepticism. The notion of conflict of interest is hardly news when for-profit firms offer programs to schools. Indeed, one rarely meets vendors who say that other programs are better than their own.

In addition, one must be aware that program developers housed in universities and other not-for-profit agencies also have strong financial interests in the success of their programs. Often their jobs and perquisites depend on continued government and foundation funding. Consider the controversy surrounding Success for All. Although its developers declare it a huge success, independent evaluators find essentially negative evidence (e.g., Slavin, 1999; Venezky, 1998). While one does not suspect dishonesty, internal evaluations can be subject to a number of biases (see Greenberg & Walberg, 1998). This is hardly a new insight. The Romans warned us long ago—"let the buyer beware."

Thus far, all three estimation approaches relied on information provided by others. However, secondary information on program effects will not always be available. Such would be the case if you developed a literacy program for your school or district. In this instance, you would have to estimate the effects of the program using your own analysis, perhaps using a pilot study. It is well beyond the scope of this chapter to undertake a detailed discussion of the various measurement strategies and instruments available to teachers and administrators. I urge readers interested in studying these strategies to consult one or more of the educational measurement texts cited at the close of this chapter (e.g., Linn & Gronlund, 1995; Popham, 2000). Nevertheless, I would like to make two important points regarding your analysis.

First, almost all literacy program objectives can serve as a basis for constructing an effectiveness measure. Indeed, one must learn to distinguish between the difficult to measure and the impossible to measure. Table 3, for example, highlights several objectives and suggests how one might measure the effects of each alternative. While this categorization certainly does not exhaust all literacy objectives, it offers several possibilities.

Secondly, there are often several ways to measure the effects of any given objective. In fact, most objectives are sufficiently complex that a single measuring instrument rarely provides ample information. For example, educators are often interested in students' attitudes toward reading (Stahl, 1999). It is highly unlikely that any one measuring instrument, such as a student survey or observational judgment, could provide a satisfactory portrayal of such attitudes. Students' attitudes are so multidimensional that it would likely take several measures to assess properly the ways students really feel about reading.

Another reason for employing multiple rather than a single measure is that few measuring devices are perfect. For example, educators often use large-scale standardized test scores as the sole measure of the effectiveness of a program. However, the common use of standardized testing obscures a rather heated debate among educators, scholars, and analysts concerning the psychometric properties of individual tests and the tests' relevance to desired educational outputs such as student learning. Tests are subject to a number of serious criticisms, such as failing to accurately measure student learning and incorporating social biases into the evaluation process. Simply put, relying on test scores only provides a distorted view how programs affect student learning.[18] Thus, when considering the effects of any alternative, educators should not opt for *the* measure. The array of information resulting from multiple measures will be more defensible and lead to better decisions.

**Table 3**
**Examples of Effectiveness Measures**

| Program Objective | What to Measure | How to Measure |
|---|---|---|
| Improving Reading Skills | Reading Skills | Test Scores:<br>1.   Absolute Levels<br>2.   Averages<br>3.   Comparative Scores<br>4.   Mastery Levels<br>5.   Achievement Gains<br>6.   Effect Sizes<br>Authentic Assessments |
| Improving Student Attitudes Toward Reading | | Attitude Scales<br>Teacher Observations |
| Improving Citizenship | Citizenship | Social Responsibility Scales<br>Consumer Behavior Inventories |
| Improving Student Retention | Student Retention | Enrollment Statistics<br>Attrition Rates<br>Repetition Rates |
| Improving Student Attainment | Student Attainment | Progression Rates<br>Graduation Rates<br>Admission to Further Study<br>Achievement in Further Study<br>Employment Statistics<br>Earnings Profiles |

## Estimating Costs

The best way to estimate the cost of each alternative is to employ what is commonly referred to as the "ingredients" method (Levin, 1983). The premise of this approach is that each alternative uses ingredients that have a cost. If one can identify the ingredients and estimate their costs, it then becomes possible to compare the total cost of each alternative.

To illustrate the ingredients method let us return to our example. In our hypothetical case, we must choose among three programs, A, B, and

---

[18] I have decided not to deal with the controversy over testing in detail. Nevertheless, it is important that educators be aware of this controversy and guard against the ready identification of test results with student learning.

C. The following briefly describes each program.

•     Program A requires that we purchase twenty-five prepackaged literacy programs for $2,000. We anticipate that the program materials (e.g., texts) will last five years.

•     Program B requires that we develop our own critical literacy program at a cost of $5,000. The program draws on parent volunteers and requires that students purchase supplemental reading materials. We anticipate that the program materials will last five years.

•     Program C requires that we purchase twenty-five computer-assisted literacy programs for $2,000. In addition, we would need to purchase twenty-five computers and a printer. We anticipate that the program materials (e.g., software, computers, and printers) will last five years.

In addition, assume that each alternative requires a teacher, a classroom, and desks.

The identification and valuation of ingredients is facilitated by dividing the ingredients into categories that have common properties. A typical breakdown would include the following categories: (a) personnel, (b) materials and equipment, (c) facilities, (d) student and parent inputs, and (e) miscellaneous inputs. Table 4 reports a set of costs that one might anticipate under each of these alternatives. In making the calculations, I used the following procedures.

*Personnel.* Personnel ingredients include all of the human resources required to provide the alternative. This category includes paid employees and consultants as well as volunteers. For full-time workers, the cost includes their salary plus fringe benefits. For part-time workers, the cost includes a percentage of their salary and benefits. I assigned a cost to the parent volunteers based on the salary of teachers' aids. Why assign a cost to volunteers? If I am unable to find enough volunteers, I will have to pay someone to carry out these duties.

*Materials and Equipment.* Materials and equipment refer to materials, furnishings, and instructional equipment that are required for each alternative. More specifically, these ingredients would include books, commercial tests, and other printed materials as well as instructional equipment (e.g., computers) and supplies. To calculate annual costs, the actual costs of these items should be divided by the number of years of anticipated use. For example, I annualized the PCs, software, printer, prepackaged materials, and internally developed materials over five years and the teacher and student desks over ten years.

*Facilities.* Facilities include the physical space to house the alternative, such as offices, classrooms, and storage areas. The cost assigned to this ingredient is typically the cost to lease a similar facility. Although these costs do not differ in our example, they often do. For example, consider the additional classroom space required by Reading Recovery.

*Student and Parent Inputs.* These costs represent the costs imposed on students and their parents. For example, Alternative B requires parents to purchase supplemental reading materials.

*Miscellaneous Inputs.* Miscellaneous inputs are those costs that do not fit easily into one of the other categories. In our example, these costs include training, insurance, and utilities.

**Table 4:**
**Cost Analysis of Critical Literacy Programs**

| Ingredients | A | B | C |
|---|---|---|---|
| Personnel: | | | |
| 1 Teacher (full-time) | $50 | $50 | $50 |
| 5 Volunteers  (20 hours per week) | | $25 | |
| Technical Support (1/10 time) | | | $5 |
| Materials and Equipment: | | | |
| 25 PCs ($7,500/5 years) | | | $1,500 |
| 25 Software ($2,000/5 years) | | | $400 |
| 1 printer ($100/5 years) | | | $20 |
| 25 Prepackaged Programs ($2,000/5 years) | $400 | | |
| 25 Internally Developed Program, ($5,000/5 years) | | $1,000 | |
| 25 Student Desks ($250/10 years) | 25 | $25 | $25 |
| 1 Teacher Desk ($250/10 years) | $25 | $25 | $25 |
| Facilities: | | | |
| 1000 sq. foot classroom | $25 | $25 | $25 |
| Parent and Student Inputs: | | | |
| Supplemental Reading ($4 per student) | | $100 | |
| Miscellaneous Inputs: | | | |
| Added Utilities | | | $50 |
| Added Insurance | | | $50 |
| Teacher Training | | | $100 |
| | | | |
| Total Annual Cost | $625 | $1,250 | $2,250 |
| Annual Cost Per Student (25 students) | $25 | $50 | $90 |

The usefulness of the ingredients approach is apparent. First, and perhaps most important, it reduces the chance of overlooking the costs associated with any given alternative. For example, Program C would likely require technical support and teacher training, costs that might be overlooked when discussing the program with a vendor. Secondly, application of the ingredients method can alert decision makers to potential problems. Under Program B, parents would have to pay $4 for supplemental reading materials. In many districts, this would be an unrealistic burden for families. Finally, once an alternative is selected, the information provided by the ingredients method allows school officials to plan for the upcoming fiscal cycle. Program C, for example, would add to the workload of the technical support team. If they have free time, this would not be a problem. However, if these additional responsibilities increase their workload beyond their capacity, a new employee would be needed. Failure to recognize this situation and plan accordingly can lead to staffing problems.[19]

## Selecting the Alternative

At this point in the process, having estimated the costs and effects of each alternative, you can now make a decision. As noted previously, your decision should not rest rigidly on the results of the analysis. The very complex nature of literacy does not lend itself to simple analyses of costs and effects.

The important point here is that teachers and administrators should use the results of the cost-effectiveness analysis to *inform*, not *dictate* decisions. Any cost-effectiveness analysis only provides information (albeit extremely useful information) that must be combined with other pertinent data in selecting an alternative.

## A Final Word

For many teachers and administrators, the task of trying to improve literacy instruction in meaningful ways is something they wrestle with daily. This task has been made all the more difficult by a growing number of environmental conditions, including the changing roles and responsibilities associated with high stakes accountability systems. Without an appropriate decision-making framework, an already difficult job becomes even more difficult.

This chapter introduced a decision-making tool that I believe can be useful to teachers and administrators. Perhaps the greatest value of cost-

---

[19] See Levin (1983) for a comprehensive discussion of the application and use of the ingredients method in educational settings.

effectiveness analysis is that it forces us to think in a disciplined manner about the costs and effects of educational programs. Judgments about costs and effects of competing programs are unavoidable, since the selection of programs, almost without exception, will be made under resource constraints and the watchful eyes of policymakers and the public. Moreover, without such an approach, educators will remain at the mercy of the hidden agendas of commercial entities.[20]

---

[20] This chapter was written for a wide audience with differing proficiencies in evaluation and cost-analysis and with differing abilities to influence curricular decisions. As such, I avoided much of the jargon and detail that characterizes most discussions of cost-effectiveness analysis in the educational setting. Those who wish to use the tools provided in this chapter are encouraged to read further. For this purpose, see the reference list at the close of this chapter.

# References

Alkin, M.C., Hofstetter, C.H., & Ai, X. (1998). Stakeholder Concepts. *Advances in Educational Productivity*, vol. 7, edited by A. J. Reynolds & H. J. Walberg, 87–113. Greenwich, CT: JAI Press Inc.

Allington, R. L. & Woodside-Jiron. H. (1999). The Politics of Literacy Teaching: How Research Shaped Educational Policy. *Educational Researcher* 28, no. 8. (pp. 4–13).

Anderson, G. L., & P. Irvine. (1993). Informing Critical Literacy with Ethnography, in *Critical Literacy: Politics, Praxis, and the Postmodern,* edited by C. Lankshear & P. L. McLaren. Albany, NY: SUNY Press. (pp. 81–104).

Anderson, R., J. Osborn, & Tierney. R. (1984). *Learning to Read in American Schools: Basal Readers and Content Texts*. Hillsdale, N.J: L. Erlbaum Associates.

Chall, J. S. (1996). American Reading Achievement: Should We Worry? *Research in the Teaching of English* 30, no. 3. (pp. 303–310).

Coulson, A. J. (1996). Schooling and Literacy Over Time: The Rising Cost of Stagnation and Decline. *Research in the Teaching of English* 30, no. 3. (pp. 311–327).

de Castell, S., & Luke, A. (1983). Defining "Literacy" in North American Schools: Social and Historical Conditions and Consequences. *Journal of Curriculum Studies.* 15. (pp. 373–389).

Edwards, W., & Newman, J. R. (1982). *Multiattribute Evaluation*. London: Sage.

Fuhrman, S. H. (1999). The New Accountability. *CPRE Policy Briefs.* (pp. 1–11, 27).

Gee, J. P., Hull, G. & Lankshear, C. (1996). *The New Work Order: Behind the Language of the New Capitalism*. Boulder Co.: Westview Press.

Gratz, D.B. (2000). High Standards for Whom? *Phi Delta Kappan* 81, no. 9. (pp. 681–687).

Greenberg, R. C. & Walberg. H. J. (1998). The Diogenes Effect: Why Program Evaluations Fail. *Advances in Educational Policy*, vol. 4, edited by K. K. Wong. Greenwich, CT: JAI Press Inc. (pp. 167–178).

Ladd, H. F., & Hansen, J. S. eds. (1999). *Making Money Matter: Financing America's Schools*. Washington, DC: National Academy Press.

Ladd, H. F., ed. (1996). *Holding Schools Accountable*. Washington, DC: The Brookings Institution.

Levin, H., (1983). *Cost-Effectiveness: A Primer.* London: Sage.

Linn, R.L. & Gronlund, N.E. (1995). *Measurement and Assessment in Teaching*. Englewood Cliffs, NJ: Merrill.

Malen, B., & Muncey, D. (2000). Creating a New Set of Givens? The Impact of State Activism on School Autonomy, in *Local Control and State Responsibility for Education*, edited by N. D. Theobald and B. Malen. Larchmont, NY: Eye on Education, Inc. (pp. 199–244).

Monk, D.H., & King, J.A. (1993). Cost Analysis as a Tool for Education Reform, in *Reforming Education: The Emerging Systemic Approach*, edited by S. L. Jacobson and R. Berne. Thousand Oaks, CA: Corwin Press, Inc. (pp. 131–152).

Nagel, S. S., & Bievenue, L. (1993). Education Policy and Multi-Criteria Decision-Making. *Advances in Educational Productivity*, vol. 3, edited by H. J. Walberg, Greenwich, CT: JAI Press Inc. (pp. 123–171).

Nas, T. (1996). *Cost-Benefit Analysis: Theory and Application.* Thousand Oaks, CA: Sage Publications.

NCES. (1999). *Projection of Education Statistics to 2009.* Washington, DC: U.S. Department of Education.

Nowakowski, J. A. ed. (1985). *Handbook of Educational Variables: A Guide to Evaluation.* Boston: Kluwer Academic Publishers.

Popham, W. J. (1999). *Classroom Assessment: What Teachers Need to Know.* Boston: Allyn and Bacon.

Popham, W. J. (1996). *Educational Evaluation.* Boston: Allyn and Bacon.

Popham, W.J. (2000). *Educational Measurement.* Boston: Allyn and Bacon.

Shannon, P. (1993). Developing Democratic Voices. *The Reading Teacher* 47. (pp. 86–94).

Shannon, P. (1987). Commercial Reading Materials, A Technological Ideology, and the Deskilling of Teachers. *The Elementary School Journal* 87 (pp. 307–329).

Shor, I. (2000). What Is Critical Literacy. *Journal for Pedagogy, Pluralism & Practice.* (pp. 1–27).

Slavin, R. E. (1999). Success for All: Policy Consequences of Replicable Schoolwide Reform. *Handbook of Educational Policy*, edited by Gregory J. Cizek. New York: Academic Press. (pp. 325–349).

Slavin, R.E. (1996). *Every Child, Every School: Success for All.* Thousand Oaks, CA: Corwin Press.

Stahl, S. A. (1999). Why Innovations Come and Go (and Mostly Go): The Case of Whole Language. *Educational Researcher* 28, no. 8. (pp. 13–22).

Stedman, L. C. (1996). An Assessment of Literacy Trends, Past, and Present. *Research in the Teaching of English* 30, no. 3. (pp. 283–302).

Venezky, R. L. (1998). An Alternative Perspective on Success for All. *Advances in Educational Policy*, vol. 4, edited by K. K. Wong. Greenwich, CT: JAI Press Inc.. (pp. 145–165).

Walberg, H. J. (1996). U.S. Schools Teach Reading Least Productively. *Research in the Teaching of English* 30, no. 3 (pp. 328–343).

# ✂ Contributors

**Brian O. Brent** is an Assistant Professor of Educational Leadership at the University of Rochester. He received his Ph.D. and M.S. degrees from Cornell University and an M.S. Degree in Taxation from Arizona State University. Professor Brent is also a certified public accountant. Brent studies issues concerning school-based financing, resource allocation and use, educational policy, teacher and administrator training, and educational productivity. Brent has written widely, publishing over twenty journal articles, book chapters, monographs, and research reports. He is also coauthor of *Raising Money for Education* (1997) with David H. Monk. Brent has also consulted for federal agencies, chief state school officers, and many local districts.

**Gerald Coles** lives in Ithaca, New York, and writes on literacy and learning. He has published articles in education, psychology, and neuropsychology journals. His 1978 *Harvard Education Review* paper on learning disabilities was cited by the Institute for Scientific Information as a "Citation Classic" because of the number of times it has been discussed in other professional papers. His two recently published books are *Reading Lessons: The Debate Over Literacy* (1998) and *Misreading Reading: How Bad Science Hurts Children* (2000). He has taught in the Department of Psychiatry at Robert Wood Johnson Medical School and the Warner Graduate School of Education and Human Development at the University of Rochester, but is glad to be an escapee from academia.

**Lynn Astarita Gatto**, an urban educator for twenty-five years, has taught all grades at the elementary level, as well as special education. Her classroom has been a demonstration site for hundreds of teachers. She is a 1997 recipient of the Presidential Award for Excellence in Mathematics and Science Teaching. She is a national presenter for educational conferences and is published in *Science and Children* and *Facts On File*. Ms. Gatto is a doctoral student in the University of Rochester's Warner Graduate School of Education.

**James Paul Gee** received his Ph.D. in Linguistics from Stanford University. He started his career in theoretical linguistics, working in syntactic and semantic theory, and taught initially in the School of

Language and Communication at Hampshire College in Amherst, Massachusetts. He went on to do research in psycholinguistics at Northeastern University in Boston and at the Max Planck Institute for Psycholinguistics in Holland. As his research focus began to switch to studies on discourse analysis, sociolinguistics, and applications of linguistics to literacy and education, he took a position in the School of Education at Boston University, where he was the chair of the Department of Developmental Studies and Counseling. From Boston University, he went on to serve as a professor of linguistics in the Linguistics Department at the University of Southern California and, later, served as the first Jacob Hiatt Professor of Education in the Hiatt Center for Urban Education at Clark University in Worcester, Massachusetts. In 1998, he became the Tashia Morgridge Professor of Reading in the Department of Curriculum and Instruction at the University of Wisconsin at Madison, the first endowed chair in reading in the United States. His books include *Sociolinguistics and Literacies* (1990, Second Edition 1996); *The Social Mind* (1992); *Introduction to Human Language* (1993); *The New Work Order: Behind the Language of the New Capitalism* (1996, with Glynda Hull and Colin Lankshear); and *An Introduction to Discourse Analysis: Theory and Method* (1999).

**Kris D. Gutierrez** is Professor of Education at UCLA's Graduate School of Education and Information Studies. Her research examines the social and cognitive consequences of literacy practices in urban school contexts and focuses on the relationship between language, culture, and learning.

**Patricia D. Irvine**, Assistant Professor at San Francisco State University, has researched literacy in Native American communities and the Eastern Caribbean. Her research focuses on understanding the impact of sociohistorical context on language learning among language minority students. She has published in *Harvard Educational Review*, *Language Arts*, and *Journal of Education*.

**Joanne Larson** is Associate Professor of Literacy and Elementary Education and chair of the Teaching and Curriculum program at the University of Rochester's Warner Graduate School of Education. She received her Ph.D. in Curriculum from UCLA's Graduate School of Education and Information Studies. Her research focuses on literacy as a social practice and examines the ways in which classroom language and literacy practices mediate access to participation in literacy events. Her publications include articles in *Research in the Teaching of English,*

*Written Communication, Linguistics and Education, Discourse and Society,* and coauthored articles in *Harvard Educational Review, Language Arts, Urban Education,* and the *International Journal of Educational Reform.*

**Patrick Shannon** is a professor of education at Penn State University. His most recent books are *text, lies & videotape* (1995), *Reading Poverty* (1998), *You'd Better Shop Around: Selling Literacy* (2000), and *Becoming Political Too* (2000). Currently, he is studying adolescents' understanding of history and social movements.

# Index

*Colin Lankshear, Michele Knobel,*
*Chris Bigum, & Michael Peters, General Editors*

New literacies and new knowledges are being invented "in the streets" as people from all walks of life wrestle with new technologies, shifting values, changing institutions, and new structures of personality and temperament emerging in a global informational age. These new literacies and ways of knowing remain absent from classrooms. Many education administrators, teachers, teacher educators, and academics seem largely unaware of them. Others actively oppose them. Yet, they increasingly shape the engagements and worlds of young people in societies like our own. The New Literacies and Digital Epistemologies series will explore this terrain with a view to informing educational theory and practice in constructively critical ways.

For further information about the series and submitting manuscripts, please contact:

Dr. Colin Lankshear
"Papeleria Garabatos"
Av Universidad #1894, Local 1
Col. Oxtopulco Universidad
Mexico City, CP 04310
MEXICO
Fax 1-508-267 1287
c.lankshear@yahoo.com

To order other books in this series, please contact our Customer Service Department at:

(800) 770-LANG (within the U.S.)
(212) 647-7706 (outside the U.S.)
(212) 647-7707 FAX

Or browse online by series at:

www.peterlangusa.com